# She's Seen...
# She's Heard...
# She's safe.

## Pippa Rafael

Faithbuilders Publishing UK

© Pippa Rafael 2025

Faithbuilders Publishing
United Kingdom

ISBN: 978-1-913181-99-4

All rights reserved. No Part of this Publication may be reproduced, stored in a retrieval system, or transmitted in any form or by any means without the prior permission of the publisher.

Unless otherwise stated all scripture reference are taken from the New King James Version®. Copyright © 1982 by Thomas Nelson. Used by permission. All rights reserved.

British Library Cataloguing in Publication Data. A catalogue record for this book is available from the British Library

Formatted by Faithbuilders Publishing
Cover concept by Ruth Holland
Printed in the United Kingdom

# Contents

Endorsements

Introduction

1. Bad Company Corrupts Good Character
2. Whose Prison?
3. Secrecy or Security
4. Mistakes v Crimes
5. Thirteen Minutes
6. One Month
7. A Shaky Decision
8. Two For the Price of One
9. Waiting
10. A Duo of Arrests
11. Layer Upon Layer
12. Rizla Paper
13. River Tay
14. On Hold
15. Take Him Down!
16. Two Angels
17. Copious Burps
18. The Stand
19. Dirty, Grotty Place
20. The Verdict

21. Sentencing
22. The Grey Van
Epilogue

# Endorsements

The reality of abuse and its consequences is far reaching. This book reveals the pain of trauma and the persistence to see justice. It also reveals the cost and strength required, not only for the victim, but to those who also have to live through it with them."

Pastor Richard Caswell
The Bridge Church

- o – o – o – o –


Pippa shares a particularly painful, powerful and courageous journey.

From enduring the trauma of childhood sexual abuse, to navigating her way through the judicial system. All the while bearing the challenging impact upon family dynamics and managing the understandable myriad of emotions.

From the shadows of debilitating silence, Pippa describes how she finds a resilience and voice.

A truly valuable resource for others facing such treacherous and challenging pathways.

Sarah Nicholson MSc
Specialist Psychotherapist
Department of Neurology

- o – o – o – o –

This personal insight and account of one's trauma and courage to confront is a read that brings you into a world of emotions and feelings that a defenceless little one endured.... Written with a unique eloquence and vulnerability. We are allowed a glimpse of something that is so painful and personal. It is an inspiring read of a little girl now a woman who survived and keeps surviving.

Darren and Julie Jones
Mattersey Hall Training Centre
Green Pastures

# Introduction

My story does not begin with this book. "I'm Alright, I'm only Hurting" was written to document my own thoughts and feelings as I struggled to process the early trauma of childhood sexual abuse. It evolved into a book that was written in 2021, long before it was available to buy three years later. Just days before it was due to be released there was an unexpected turn of events, requiring the CPS to put a hold on it whilst a criminal investigation took place.

So, this is the next part of my journey as I navigate and reposition my life from a place of pain and the aftermath of childhood sexual abuse by a family member and others. The little girl of the past has lived inside me for so many years, but now I see her growing, attempting to leave behind her fears, and stepping into new shoes, which are still painful and often feel like they don't fit. The necessity of unpicking the fragmented pieces of my mind and soul have led me into new territory.

At the onset of this healing journey, and for many years afterwards, I had had no intention to prosecute or fully hold to account the men who had damaged me, yet here I was, finding myself doing just that. Here, in this book, are my thought processes, challenges, doubts, alongside the unfolding of the truth being told, and the way that justice was served.

# Chapter One
## Bad Company Corrupts Good Character

The curious case of Benjamin Button came to mind. A man who started his life as an old man and wound up an infant at the end of his life.

That, in a strange way, was how I felt. As I got older in age, the little girl within seemed to rise, and my adult logic was compromised by the challenges I had encountered as a small child. My past was having an effect on me that wasn't maturing me, but rather was creating a regression that paraded itself before me with increasing intensity when I didn't want it or least expected it.

I had certainly been blessed by a mum and dad who deeply loved me and built around me a bubble-wrap-like world that consisted of God, wholesome company, and to think about buttercups and daisies when days were blue.

It was a stable home for Joey and me, with huge amounts of love and affection. He was five years older than me and as humble as humanly possible. As he got older, he was deeply embarrassed at references of him being like an action man. He had a chiselled jaw and a hair style that he spent more time on than his homework. As I got older, I'm sure my friends didn't come over for my choice of entertainment as I could see them unable to steal themselves away from as many glances at him as they thought they could get away with. Joey, who didn't reciprocate their feelings in the slightest, would just disappear out of sight as quickly as possible.

Dad and Joey were cut from the same cloth; neither considered themselves good looking, both were shy, and they would always put the other person first. If there were six pieces of cake and the plate went round five people, they would always let it go round again, ensuring everyone had more than enough before taking one themselves. It always made me laugh as I couldn't fathom their logic. There was enough cake, so just take a piece!

Our home was a little different to a lot of homes...well, the ones I knew anyway...especially at night. Through no fault of their own, Mum and Dad and poor Joey had to plan their life around my breathing problems. I had severe nocturnal brittle asthma, the effects of which spilled into the next day, leaving the household exhausted from the upheaval of doctors' visits, steaming kettles, and often an ambulance arriving on the doorstep. From six months old, I'd been bundled off to hospital without my parents, and I grew to resign myself to the situation. However, I did not realise its impact until I was grown up.

When I was eighteen months old, I was given a vaccine that triggered cowpox by a nurse who was uneducated in the dos and don'ts of what brittle asthmatics can tolerate. I ended up in Birmingham isolation hospital and, to Mum and Dad's horror, chickens we're running around the grounds, chaotically bashing and flapping their wings at the windows. After a week of battling for my life, I then had salmonella food poisoning!

I remember crying for Mummy, who couldn't stay, as I was put in isolation in an oxygen tent, desperately wanting

Lacey, my cloth comforter, that had been forgotten in all the chaos.

"Oh, Mrs Mallard, stop crying! If she dies, you can always have another one," came the abrupt comment from a rather rattled and overworked cleaner. Mum told this story with a fresh, appalled indignance, every time.

Just as a Christmas dinner is referred to as having all the trimmings, so was my health. "Oh. she has asthma, eczema and allergies." I used to think it sounded like a starter, main course, and dessert.

The world in which my mum and dad had carefully placed me, turned out to be one that had secrets. Not their secrets, but my own. They had trusted, albeit naively, almost everyone in my life. The ones they didn't, Mum quickly severed contact, including relatives if she thought they would lead me and Joey astray. "Bad company corrupts good character!" was her mantra, which I completely agreed with. However, someone's bad character is not always evident, and in my case, I learnt that the hard way as a little girl of six years old.

There was no secrecy in the fact that my Uncle Dick led a crooked life. In the dead of night, Uncle Dick would break into the local grocery store and lower himself down, bundling he loaded his bags with tinned fruit and large joints of meat until they hung to the floor. When he got home, Auntie Mavis's job was to take all the labels off so no one knew where they were from, and in case the police raided them. The downside of it was that you didn't know whether you were opening tinned peaches or red salmon. Apparently, one night, she tried to hide the biggest piece of beef behind the settee, and she said it had one eye open, looking at her. I believed it, of course!

Mum didn't like to admit that she saw the funny side of the stories, so with what appeared to be true conviction (and a smidge of religiosity thrown in), she distanced us from that side of the family so that I would not be 'led astray'.

Therefore, I grew up spending lots of time with my lovely Uncle Ray and Auntie Iris. They were my favourite aunt and uncle. Uncle Ray was a local lay preacher whose stories were not saturated with crime, but tales of life, death and the antics of church leaders and parishioners; just as fascinating and, at times, rather eye-opening!

Which then left my Uncle Ivan and Auntie Glenda. Mum was especially close to her sister, and Uncle Ivan tagged along when he was home from his trips abroad. In Mum's eyes, there was no reason to believe anything but what she saw in front of her. Two respectable relatives, including a sister she loved, who were both law-abiding and weren't uncouth in any way, shape, or form. Auntie Glenda always showed an interest in God and often went along to church with us, to the delight of my mum. She would often sing hymns loudly in the bathroom, which I always thought of as attention-seeking as she never sang them at any other time.

In the summer of 1976, however, my life changed when I went to stay for two weeks on my own at Uncle Ivan and Auntie Glenda's. Mum and Dad would certainly be able to catch up on some much-needed sleep, and Joey would finally get some one-on-one time.

I was nervous about going. Leaving home was something that had been enforced on me for much of my life, through no fault of anyone's. Uncountable hospital stays had become something I had resigned myself to, but each visit just added to the impact of the previous one.

I knew all too well what separation was and what anxiety felt like, but I had no idea that it was a 'thing' until years later. Social work taught me that one. Now, as I care for young children in the world of fostering, I have first-hand understanding of the depth of trauma that is caused by separation anxiety in children who are taken away from the one who provides their care, nurture and stability. Its effects can be devastating, and it can take a huge amount of love, nurture and security to heal it. Equally, children I have cared for who have never had those attachments, can doubly suffer as they become lost in their own world of confusion, because their attachments are warped, and they still feel the anxiousness of separation.

Auntie Glenda had no idea, at that time, of the trauma that I was silently going through because of illness and insecurities, but neither did my mum or dad. I loved them all so much, and I never wanted to hurt them or make them angry or upset with me.

To my utter horror, Uncle Ivan became the type of man no one would want their child to be nearby. On that holiday, he started to touch me and make me touch him. He was in his forties, which to me was ancient, and it made it even more repugnant. The rapid transition of going from trusting someone I loved to fearing them beyond belief was almost too much to bear. He took every opportunity to get away with as much as he could during that holiday, all the time knowing that I was unwell, quiet, and vulnerable.

I had no one to turn to and no one to protect me. He had his perfect prey and, all the time, he flew under the radar of Auntie Glenda and Mum and Dad's attention. As I grew, other people in my life failed to notice the changes and insecurities in me, too. There were so many changes in me, from that point, but the illness masked every one of them.

As I navigated my childhood, insult was added to injury as there were repeats and escalations of Uncle Ivan's sexually predatory behaviour towards me, culminating in my final devastating holiday with him at fourteen years of age.

That time, I had gone with some cousins who were around the same age as me. Clearly, they were not encountering Uncle Ivan's attention as they laughed, were constantly at the park, and were happily climbing the hills of Scotland around Auntie's house. I had noticed how quickly they were both able to fall asleep, at peace after a fun-filled day, whilst I would bite down hard on my quilt to cause the gut-wrenching crying to be silenced. Thank goodness I had been in my own bed! I had cried to Jesus and desperately prayed that he would help me and rescue me whilst a cascade of chaotic and desperate thoughts had tried to make sense of that night's horrific attention from Uncle Ivan, all while trying to override the mental anguish of the fear of what tomorrow's encounters would bring.

I had been sworn to secrecy by him, and life had embedded in me the skill to bear something alone, without showing anyone around that I was hurting. Hence the naming of my first book: 'I'm alright, I'm only hurting'. I had done it for those I loved, and also for self-preservation. If nobody knew, then no one would be in trouble, and I wouldn't be guilty of hurting my family. I had thought it was my duty to protect Auntie, and I'd promised Uncle Ivan too, so, to a degree, I felt I owed him, too. I had a secret that Uncle Ivan made me promise I would never tell.

He carried on as if nothing had happened. How could he chat to my Mum and Dad and look in their eyes? I couldn't, and I belonged to them! I felt sad, ashamed and scared that this awful secret would be released and eat me up alive if I let my guard down. Little did I realise that this constant reinforcement of wrong thinking blurred boundaries and caused an internalising of fear, pain, and self-hatred.

As a child and young person, I had then become prey to other adults' sexual misconducts. Not only was I unsafe with family, but I was also unsafe at church, yet I desperately tried to believe the best in everyone. However, the string of memories I chose to bury had a mind of their own, and all of them clubbed together and surfaced when I least expected them.

# Chapter Two
## Whose Prison?

If only the day would pass by quicker and let me get alone into my studio, my haven, my place where my thoughts come together, and I could start to create another work of art. Geoff had happily created this room for me - drilling, hanging ever-increasing pieces of art and creations that always surprised me each time I looked at them. After all the years of illness, I'd certainly developed my own style and, more often than not, hands-down acknowledged that it was a gift from God and that I needed His help with drawing each one. Being self-taught, I often did not know what or which technique to use, and heavily relied on my scrap piece of paper by my side...and a lot of prayer.

My solace; my place of peace. I pondered on this. That was the ideal...and if only it truly was. On the one hand, I revelled in the knowledge of having my own little studio and place to pray, but how many hours turned out to not be that at all! Earphones on, pencil in hand, a cup of tea (on tough days, a glass of wine at arms-length), and off I went, embarking on the next stage of my present drawing or commission in hand.

I had always lost myself in worship to the Lord, and having my new earphones meant the rest of the household was a long way away and it was just me, Jesus and, unfortunately, my pain.

As soon as I started to talk to Jesus, the tears would start. "Oh no! Goodness me! I can't get them on my drawing!" The mascara would ruin it, and it wouldn't be the first picture I'd had to abandon as it reached its tear-ridden demise.

Sitting back to compose myself, I resigned myself to another evening that was evidently going to be a repeat of so many others that had gone before. The vulnerability and raw honesty that comes out of any genuine time spent with God had inevitably caused the pain in my heart to bubble up, and the little girl that still felt alone inside me crept to the surface. I needed so desperately to soothe her and convince her that it wouldn't always be like this.

Who was I kidding? People have glass in them for years after an accident! I had even seen pictures of people who were struck by lightning whose jewellery was burnt into their skin tissue, and it remained years later. Well, that was obviously me, too! I felt angry and let down. Yes, angry at myself, and deeply disappointed in the fact that I was that one who couldn't find freedom.

Picking my phone up, I went to message my friends, Ann and Rob. They were always there to reassure me or just listen to my barmy rants. God had provided me with them. Even I was exhausted with me, so I dreaded to think how they felt after supporting me in the last few years. "Nope!" I said to myself and put the phone back down. "It's pointless, what can they do? What can anyone do? Not even God is setting me free!"

I was at rock bottom. Abandoning my drawing, I sat back on my chair with a deep, heart-wrenching gulp of emotion. "I'm in this prison and I just have to accept it. I have a life sentence and it's over, the fight for freedom is over! I'm IN PRISON!"

Prison! Bars! Guilt! Life sentence! Again, guilt! Whose guilt? "Hang on…I didn't choose to hurt me," I pondered! "I had been a little girl; just an ordinary, plain little girl. Uncle Ivan had made a choice to hurt me and then went on to repeat it over and over again." My tears started to dry up. It was like a huge quilt was being rolled back and the daylight was flooding in.

The sexual abuse I had suffered was NOT my fault, and I definitely was not the one who should be in prison! I had never ever thought of that before. God had blessed me with a very forgiving heart, and I had carried many damaging things in my heart, but unforgiveness was never one of them.

If I'm not the one who's guilty or should be in prison, then it's Uncle Ivan who is guilty! Therefore, he should be the one who must give an account of the choices he made. He committed the crimes and caused the wounds that I had to carry as if nothing had ever happened. He created a world around him and me that caused denial, and he had no thoughts of the consequences or pain or how that world would grow.

But hang on…I can't do this! Look at me! Who do I think I am…!

Thoughts of talking to the police were like little, tiny rain drops, landing in my soul. Each one another question. Could I? Should I? What if? But…? Would they believe me? Is what happened really that bad?

It was the end of my supposedly productive art session, and I jumped as I looked up to see two eyes peering at me, and a tap on my studio window beckoned me to let them in.

There she was...my friend Ann, who seemed to have an internal radar and crept up upon me with stealth every time I reached rock bottom.

It was a Sunday evening, and a night I won't forget. Something had changed and shifted in my thinking. As I sobbed and explained the life sentence that I had been given, I could not escape the new feelings and inclinations to dare to entertain thoughts that it was my uncle - the perpetrator - who should be the one standing to give an account, and that the prison I felt I was in was not the place in which I should be living. What Uncle Ivan had done was his choice and maybe, just maybe, the police would want to know about those choices. A ball had started rolling.

# Chapter Three
## Secrecy or Security

Game shows are not for me. All those questions coming thick and fast on all sorts of subjects highlight the fact that my general knowledge leaves something to be desired. I can switch the TV off at the flick of a switch, but the questions in my head... that's another matter. Oh, how I wished I had a mental remote controller! Each new question I pondered triggered a whole new reel of enquiries that certainly could not be answered in one go.

My ponderings were edging me towards bringing into the open the trauma that Uncle Ivan had put me through. I was becoming increasingly aware that the huge dark secret I'd carried for so long had been kept deeply hidden. And the last people I wanted to let see it were my closest family, never mind the rest of the world! They now knew that something had happened, but the details - and its impact on my mind and emotions - I had kept well and truly locked away.

The act of sharing such a secret felt utterly alien, and a betrayal. I would be betraying myself, as I took my own word seriously and had promised never to tell. My dad had drilled into me that my word should be my bond! It was rather an old-fashioned term but, somehow, it had a real ring of seriousness to it. Plus, all the shame and embarrassment that hung onto such a story would highlight all of Uncle Ivan's biggest mistakes...which included me. No one wants their rotten, ugly actions paraded before all and sundry. He would certainly feel betrayed and that, in turn, would make me even more guilty.

I had shared my heart to Rob and Ann and, on several occasions afterwards, had felt so wrong for having done so. The fact I had also messaged so many times back and forth, thrashing through this awful topic, caused great concern as it was written down. Now there was an account of it…and a brutally honest one at that. At least verbal a conversation is only remembered by the hearer and God; and, of course, the enemy of our souls.

There is a power and a chain attached to secrecy. The promise not to tell, and the guilt of sharing each new facet of the trauma, caused an instant sense of panic, guilt and regret, so the facility to 'delete' and 'delete for everyone' on our group chat with Rob and Ann made my oversized panic breathe a sigh of relief. It was not long before they picked up on this and could see that that button was becoming overused.

Rob, in one of his moments of sharing a Pearl of wisdom, said, "Pippa, your sharing with us, isn't secrecy; it's security. You are sharing these things and leaving them in a safe place." There was something profound in that thought.

In the past, although the secrecy had felt wrong, it was also necessary to avoid feelings of betrayal and shame in front of other people. However, opening up and sharing my secrets felt equally wrong, but I had to trust that it was necessary in order to bring me to a place of safety and security.

To put openness and security alongside each other, as though they were friends, was a new concept to me. It was Uncle Ivan's secret and nothing he said had ever made me feel secure. In fact, many times in the past, my attempt to uncover the secret had caused more problems than it was worth.

For the first time, I was beginning to understand what the Bible says in Luke: '...*whatever is spoken in the dark will be heard in the light*' (Luke 12:3). In other words, secrets will be uncovered, and truth will come into the light. Jesus' clear message is that the truth will set you free. I had shared the truth, regardless of its ugliness, and the very act of doing so was building a place of safety.

It was at that point that I made the choice to totally trust them with guarding that truth for me, even if that was written down on our WhatsApp chat. I went on to delete what I found hard to read afterwards but they kept it as a point of reference, and to remind me, in the future, of all the questions and battles that I had faced and still needed more time and help with.

## Chapter Four
## Mistakes v Crimes

The whole idea of Uncle Ivan's 'mistakes' actually being a crime was not only obvious to everyone around me, but those same people could not see his crimes as mistakes.

My own view on such crimes against children was that they were not only detestable but inconceivable, and I certainly did not view such things as mistakes. However, there seemed to be ONE exception. I could only see what Uncle Ivan did to me as somehow something different and not to be put in the same category as criminal, but rather a huge mistake, especially because of his acknowledgment that he was sorry for its effect on me and, in fact, that it had happened at all.

Was he sorry for what he'd done? Had he only said sorry in order to manipulate my silence...or had he just been paving the way to repeat his actions, which could all be clubbed together afterwards under one big apology? After all, he had always blamed me for triggering his feelings in the first place and, in Uncle Ivan's eyes, somehow the abuse that had happened to him as a ten-year-old boy had excused him from the inability to refrain from acting on his urges towards me as a six-year-old girl. I seemed to have taken this on board as an exception to the rule. Somehow, his sorry counted for something, even though I wasn't sure of its motive.

My focus was all on his feelings and responses, and rarely on how these hurt and damaged me. In all honesty, I refused to see each particular sex act or touch as a real one but just a fumbled attempt which, in my mind, made them less serious and almost excusable.

During my chats with Rob and Ann, this became evident very early on. Of course, where a crime has been committed, especially one against a child, it is a normal response to consider whether the police should be involved or not. However, the first sniff of this concept caused me to become instantly defensive and utterly objectionable to what I thought was an inconceivable suggestion. Rob and Ann were deadly serious. In my mind, firstly it had happened forty-plus years ago and secondly, Uncle Ivan was now an old infirm man. Thirdly, I had no substantial evidence and fourthly, everyone would be so angry at me and at the catastrophic consequences of such a revelation. Never ever had I entertained the slightest thought of going to the police after it happened...and had never considered it for many years afterwards.

I recall, at fourteen years of age, the police being called by the hospital staff after I'd blurted out in the middle of the night, during an allergic reaction, that my uncle was having sex with me, causing a cascade of professionals to descend and my mum and dad to be called. I was neither prepared for this, nor willing to say another word on the subject. This had blurted out of my mouth in a moment when my guard was lowered during an emotional reaction in a medical emergency. No matter how hard my mum and the police had desperately tried to extract information, my mouth had been firmly shut. I had been shocked and ashamed by my own unplanned disclosure.

So here I was with my friends all these years later, still ashamed and unprepared to tell the police, regardless of whether or not they thought it was the right thing to do. Although this was historic abuse, Ann and Rob were concerned about any possible danger that Uncle Ivan may still pose to children and young people in his family and among friends. After much conversation, we agreed that his own children and grandchildren were grown up now and they all, in fact, lived many miles away and rarely saw him. Through my ongoing relationship with Auntie Glenda, I had gleaned the fact that their family wasn't close, for whatever reason. Also, because of his illness and old age, I had a level of assurance that his previous predatory behaviours would not be given any opportunity to recur.

Auntie Glenda's overbearing, all-consuming attitude to relationships kept the other family members and remaining friends at bay, thus giving me and, in return Rob and Ann, a level of confidence that he was not posing a direct risk to children. Albeit an obvious crime to them, it was going to take a relentless amount of repetition and convincing for me to see how wrong Uncle Ivan's actions were against me.

The thoughts of anything half as bad happening to my children filled me with dread and an overwhelming anger, but there seemed to be a link missing for me to equate Uncle Ivan's squalid thoughts and actions towards me as being a crime and intentional. In my mind, he had not planned it, and his patience and gentle momentum was a demonstration of the fact he loved me. The very mention of it being 'grooming' made me instantly want to stick up for him. Grooming is what evil, manipulative, sexually depraved men do to wear their victims down into a false sense of security, leaving them vulnerable, unsure of what is happening and completely defenceless.

"That wasn't what happened to me!" I exclaimed, in no uncertain terms. To suggest that Uncle Ivan was that man made me feel panicky and wrong. The guilt was incredibly misplaced, and Rob and Ann spent the coming months tediously presenting to me the real owner of these guilty crimes: not a little girl but a fully-grown forty-year-old uncle, now a man in his eighties, who had never acknowledged them or tried to mend the grievous damage that he had done.

## Chapter Five
## Thirteen Minutes

Only one person knew why Uncle Ivan had decided to hurt me (or 'help' me, as he described it). Only he knew why I had been chosen and if he ever wished he hadn't gone ahead with his plans to sexually abuse me. No amount of surmising and trying to interpret his actions fully resolved the questions and difficulties I had in trying to understand him. So, after another rather troubled unpicking of ideas round the workings of Uncle Ivan's mind, I decided the best thing was to ring him and talk to him about it.

There was no point in telling anyone because I would lay myself wide open to people's opinions and reasons why this was not a good idea. After all, how could he hurt me? He would not be there in person; it was just a phone call. It certainly would not affect anyone else, and it was my chance to thrash through 'the subject' for which I had spent my life trying to get answers.

The last time I had had the bravery to broach the subject with him was in my early twenties. So now seemed the right time, twenty-nine years later! There had never been even a hint of talk about 'the subject' during the years of our paths crossing, and I was sure that, from his perspective, this subject was long-buried and forgotten about. Little did he know that it rumbled beneath the surface for me on almost a daily basis. The volcano that had never had the atmospherics to erupt was now letting out its lava and I couldn't get it back. It felt like it was burning a hole in me.

This phone call was definitely not a thought-out, precisely planned event, but a spur-of-the-moment decision which gave me no opportunity to back out. I needed God's help and His approval. I knew I had it as I knew that He always knows my heart's genuine reasoning behind it.

This was to find out nothing but the truth, but I had to try to be gracious as I knew it was the only approach I could take. I needed to be polite and chirpy, letting him know everything was fine. It would certainly surprise him, getting a random call from me, and I did not want to freak him out and cause him to clam up. After all, I needed as much information as I could get. It felt like this was my one and only chance to get some honest conversation going as to why all the abuse had taken place all those years ago.

Moments before I rang him, I had the idea to ask him to ring me on my landline. Then, I quickly reasoned, I could record it on my mobile and I'd have it forever, to contemplate on and try to understand the answers that he gave...maybe even hear how sorry he was to help me to move forward in the future.

I had a plan!

It worked. I found myself trembling, yet talking, and asking questions that made me squint my eyes with awkwardness, all the time recording what was being said. My toes were being squeezed and released at a rapid pace to try to regulate my irrational feelings. How could I, in my late forties, quake in my boots at the sound of his voice, yet here I was being brave...not only talking with him but actually talking about the hideous things he put me through.

I found myself listening to what appeared to be a genuine man, explaining why he did what he did to me, as if any reasoning made it okay! "You see, Pippa, you triggered me off."

I instantly, had no defences. What could I say? He certainly sounded confident in his memory of it. All I remembered doing was seeing the hairs on his legs and stroking them as an inquisitive six-year-old! Surely that wasn't wrong! It wasn't to me at the time.

Uncle Ivan quickly appeared to shift the blame, explaining how I had gone a bit too high but then added that he shouldn't have reacted. A bit too high!

"I don't remember that!" I thought, with indignation. But here I was, unable to challenge that. After all, what did I know? I had only been six years old.

"Why did you choose me? What did I do wrong? What was wrong with me?" I asked, questions rolling one after the other.

"You did nothing wrong, Pippa. It was something that happened to me when I was ten and you triggered me off."

"Did that make it alright?" I thought to myself. I was unable to defend myself or give a good enough response. He took the opportunity and moved on quickly.

"Pippa, there's nothing wrong with you. You've done nothing wrong." This totally confused me, and it was not what I expected to hear. To me, this was him owning his mistakes but, unbeknown to me at the time, he was manipulating me into minimising what had really happened. By saying I'd done nothing wrong, it took the focus off him. In fact, every reference about my part in it meant neither of us seriously highlighted the depravity of what he chose to do.

I floundered as I could see Uncle Ivan transferring his guilt and justifying his reaction towards me as a perfectly understandable thing to do in this situation.

"Hang on," I thought to myself. "What about the fact that you kept repeating your sexual advances and actions towards me and with increasing seriousness? Incidents of abuse were not only repeated, but they also escalated into rape." Uncle Ivan was clearly in denial and did everything he could to convince me that everything was ok and that what happened should not have happened, whilst trying to justify it by paralleling it to his own abuse by his babysitter.

His repetition of, "Sorry, Pippa," appeared genuine to me, but what was he saying sorry for? Sorry that it had happened? He seemed to have an excuse at every turn. Or was he just sorry that I'd brought it up again?

At the time, I'd believed it to be genuine. Over time, though, as I have replayed and scrutinised the phone call, I can see his complete lack of empathy and shifting of the blame, revealing his total lack of understanding and unwillingness to see the gravity of the crimes he had committed.

Every time I had tried to explain how his actions had affected me, he quickly responded by wanting to know how. I had instantly felt my throat close up, and all I had been able to say was, "It's really hard for me to talk about." I repeated this line several times, to my disdain, as I was desperate to tell him about some of the devastation that he had caused but found myself unable to explain. I had felt like I would make a fool of myself by voicing such things, and he would, in a clever and very convincing way, either try to explain away what I said as being gross exaggeration or totally misinterpret it.

Our thirteen minute and twenty-five second call was only ever intended to be for my ears, but it would prove to be a conversation that would play a crucial part in the next phase of my journey.

## Chapter Six
## One Month

My method of decision-making is a little unusual. I could go out to Sainsbury's garage down the road, stand in the chocolate aisle and choose five chocolate bars, pick them up and then mentally grade them from favourite to the least favourite. I would taste them in my mind's eye and then start to put them back one by one before arriving at my choice for the day; but then I would question it and start all over again.

I could stand there for so long that I had to wave past the long queue of people that had built up behind me, saying, "Go ahead as I am still deciding!" This applies to all minor and insignificant decisions I make. I take so long to decide.

However, if anyone were to ask me if I should buy a particular bed / headboard / mattress / house / car, or choose a holiday, or make any other big important decision, I can decide in moment. Ok, maybe not a moment, but within a very short space of time, with the added bonus of having no regrets afterwards.

So, here I found myself faced with one of the biggest decisions of my life:

*Do I report to the police the things Uncle Ivan did to me?*

This presented itself as a question that I could not answer in a quick, decisive fashion like the holiday I had just booked to Majorca in just thirty minutes.

For the first time ever, I could hardly believe that I was actually allowing myself to consider whether there was an ounce of a possibility that it could be the right thing to do. The cascading effects of such a decision would inevitably land on my own family, my wider family and, in return, Uncle Ivan and Auntie Glenda's family. How could such a decision be right before God and right for me personally when it would undoubtedly cause devastation, pain and change? Change that would redefine who I was and my place amongst my cousins and change that would shake up every relationship within my family, causing everyone to examine their own motives and position on such a revelation.

This was real and it was like I was holding a hand grenade in my hands. I could stand still and hold onto it, and nothing would happen, just like the previous forty-five years. But, if I were to pull that pin, the whole place would need to run for cover.

I felt a weight of responsibility. I had the power to change the course of life of everyone who was close to me or Uncle Ivan.

Despite all these feelings, I could not handle the thought of doing nothing and leaving things as they were, which was to let Uncle Ivan, who was now in his eighties, die in peace with his secrets. This would inevitably mean that I would have to bury forever the effects and emotional disability that paralysed me from Uncle Ivan's actions.

Was either decision fair? No!

Would there be any winners? No...none!

Either way, the effects would be shocking and damaging, and the amount of loss and grief that would have to be endured would be heartbreaking.

Regardless of all this, a fierce intensity of wilfulness and intransigence was becoming rooted in me.

How could I be a fierce defender of my inner six-year-old, whilst having a genuine compassion for my abuser?

"Okay, so here it is, Father!" I continually talked to God about this dilemma. He knew my deepest pain, but He also knew, in His wisdom, the way forward which I could not see. I was struggling to hear His voice, too. "Father, I'm Yours and I know Your voice. Your sheep hear Your voice."

Hearing His heart for a situation was not normally something I struggled with. In the centre of my chest, I had a spiritual barometer. It was my 'knower'; my sensor; my peace. With everything in my life, I always relied on this place - the seat in my heart where the Holy Spirit resided. So many times, I lay a question or a difficulty down at His feet, waiting for His unction. It was all I needed. Nothing surpassed the will of God, and nothing could give more meaning to my life than His plans and purposes.

I needed God's approval, but I knew this was a decision that only I could make as it would be me who had to follow it all through with determination, regardless of other people's viewpoints and opinions.

I rang Rob and Ann. "Can we meet up? I urgently need to discuss my emotional wranglings!"

It was the back end of the Covid days and face masks, and distancing was still part of everyday life. Rob especially needed his space to protect himself as he was particularly vulnerable. I did not want to compromise his health, but I needed perspective, and I needed it quickly.

We met up in the dark, one chilly evening, and sat on a moss-ridden bench, spaced apart and ready to thrash through this subject. I had arrived, all guns blazing, ready to explain why I wanted to go ahead and report Uncle Ivan. I wanted to do it immediately before anyone tried to change my mind.

It became very clear that although my reasonings to involve the law were totally valid and acceptable, this was going to take an immense amount of emotional strength and resolve. Was I strong enough and how would I cope with the myriad unforeseen challenges and deeply distressing things as the police questioned and delved into my deepest darkest times, reliving what Uncle Ivan did to me.

"You need to give yourself a time period to decide," said Ann, with Rob agreeing. It was the best thing, we decided.

*A month!*

That was it! That time was going to be spent looking at every possible scenario and difficulty. I needed to be brutally honest and look, face on, at how I would cope and handle myself in the darkest of times and under the scrutiny of the law.

How would I cope when the police categorised the crimes? Would they underestimate what I was saying, or would they view things worse than I did?

Not only that, but there was the possibility of Uncle Ivan winning and the whole thing being turned on its head, with him being found 'not guilty' and me being left defeated. Or how would I cope with the thoughts of Uncle Ivan being locked up, separated from his family, scared, and possibly even abused by the institution that should keep him safe? How would I survive if I heard he'd been brutally, sexually reprimanded in the most heinous ways by other prisoners... but I guess he'd encounter feelings similar to the ones I'd felt as a vulnerable, terrified six-year-old.

Also, how would I handle the thought of Auntie Glenda's pain? What would my resolve be, and what would I hold onto in order to keep me focused enough to see this through, because once I started the ball rolling, there would be no stopping it!

Auntie's words rang in my ears: "Don't you ever tell anyone this, especially the police. If you do, we will end our lives!"

As extreme as it sounded, it was something that I had to face, as that was always a possibility. Many paedophiles, who are accused and become defendants, end their lives at various stages of the criminal justice process. Some just before trial, others midway through, or once they start their prison sentence. Is this something I could bear?

We all agreed...a month it was! Time to thrash through all my pros and cons to come to the right decision: the decision that sat well with me and with my heart before God. I knew He was a multi-faceted God who was not just a God of love, but of righteousness and justice.

# Chapter Seven
## A Shaky Decision

How does a person weigh up whether it's right or wrong to give the approval for the demise of a family member? That's what, in essence, it felt like it would be. In fact, not just Uncle Ivan's demise, but Auntie Glenda's and their kids: my cousins. Cousins I cared about. They had done absolutely nothing wrong but were in the unfortunate position of being the grown-up kids of the uncle who couldn't keep his hands to himself. They would all have to live and contend with the stigma of being associated with a paedophile and, worse than that, a child rapist.

*Why should they suffer, and why should Auntie Glenda?*

There was no getting away from the fact that his actions couldn't be held to account in isolation, without having any effect on his nearest and dearest.

I had already distanced myself from Auntie Glenda some months before as I'd had to make a stance, making it clear that I could not tolerate any more conversations about Uncle Ivan. I certainly didn't want to see any more photos with his proud, puffed-out chest and his smile that had lots of charisma which, for me, evoked gut-wrenching memories of his sordid behaviour.

Auntie knew. She knew Uncle Ivan had done stuff. That was my word to describe what he did: *stuff*. I liked it as it didn't say anything, but it said enough. It made what happened seem smaller - less serious - and certainly did not give it a title that would instantly make me feel ashamed.

So, this *stuff*. Would Auntie Glenda understand why the police should know about it? She certainly knew something sexual had happened, but I had not embellished her with all the details. Would my cousins ever know what the *stuff* really was? I guess I had to accept that if I were to talk to the police, then they would want to know as much as I could tell them in detail...and then...would it be possible that Auntie might find out about *everything*? Most probably! The thought filled me with dread, but surely Uncle Ivan's secrets should not stay unexplained and private!

The guilt surely had to fall with Uncle Ivan. If I were to tell the police what he'd done, then I had to relinquish what I thought was my part in it...my guilt. But what *was* my part in these dreadful incidents? I had no grounds for that guilt as I had not chosen to be assaulted. I had not wanted any part of it; in fact, I had spent my whole life detesting every element of what had happened. Yet I carried guilt. An invisible, unreasonable, huge load of it. Surely, I must have done *something* wrong!

Was it the freeze mode my body went into? Rather than understanding that it was my brain's way of protecting me, I grew up automatically thinking that was the guilty part in me...that part that remained right in the middle of the incident: a recipient of his actions and unable to remove myself.

However, there was a dawning during this month, regardless of my complex feelings. I came to understand that I had been a vulnerable six-year-old little girl when it all started, and the guilt was one hundred percent his. What had I known about such things? Nothing! I was leaning towards the fact the police would probably think exactly the same thing too. This was more than *stuff*. It was serious sexual abuse, manipulation, and worthy of a police investigation.

My aunties and my only other remaining uncle were in their eighties, and some were approaching their nineties. I could not see any benefit in any of them learning, at this stage of their life, what Auntie Glenda's husband had been up to. In the past, it had given me a sense of relief that at least a few precious family members could escape learning about the sordid actions of Uncle Ivan and that they would be saved the shame of having a convicted paedophile in their family.

One cousin, in particular, really mattered to me. I had loved her all my life, regardless of the fact that I'd hardly spent any time with her. My mum had carved out a different life - a Godly one - and she, in her partial naivety, had kept us busy in our church life to the exclusion of others who did not share the same faith. As she put it, she wanted us 'grounded and rooted' in our faith and did not want 'the ways of the world' to influence us.

Mum always knew of my love for Jenny and always talked so fondly of her. Jenny was pretty, had an infectious laugh, and I thought she was so very funny. She brimmed with confidence and common sense. She had thick, long hair that swished, whereas I, on the other hand, had mousey, fine hair that Mum insisted on trimming up with a bow, and had to be fastened in like a tent that had to be bolted to the floor. Jenny had something very special about her. She was the cousin who cared, listened, and would do whatever she could in her power to help, especially as she grew older. It became evident that she could be trusted and relied upon.

Now I was facing this big decision, I knew I had to talk with Jenny. After all, she and Claire had been present all those years ago on that dreadful holiday in Scotland when Uncle Ivan had singled me out. I didn't believe Jenny or Claire knew anything at the time, but I did know that if I talked with Jenny now, she might be able to help in some way.

I was delighted to meet with them and my Auntie Kate who had prepared a feast 'fit for a king', in my mother's words. She knew how to lay on a spread! Once we had washed it down with lots of tea, we got down to why I really went to see them.

Could they remember anything at all about the holiday that we'd had together years ago at Auntie Glenda's and Uncle Ivan's? Were they aware of anything unusual or alarming that had happened? It was difficult because I did not want to give away too much information in case they did remember something and it could be used by the police if I were to put them forward as witnesses, but I also needed to give some context so that they knew what I was talking about.

I was already aware that Jenny knew that something had happened because I had talked with her about it over a Chinese meal when we were both eighteen. I asked her if she remembered this conversation. Although she could not remember the details, she could remember that something had happened with Uncle Ivan. And she and Claire had noticed some unusual activity while on the holiday, such as the doors being locked when they were outside and I was inside with Uncle Ivan, meaning that they could not get in when they needed the toilet, and that I always seemed mardy and upset and was often not out playing with them.

It was an emotional evening, and I asked them if they would be willing to be witnesses, should it be needed. Little did I know that Auntie Kate wasn't well, and I left her that night, unaware that I would never see her again. She said goodbye that night saying, "Pippa, what happened to you was very, very wrong. The Lord will be with you and help you!" I held this dear to my heart and still do.

It wasn't long before I found myself at my other auntie's funeral and only a short time later Auntie Kate, who had given me her love and approval, had also passed away. My cousins were all devastated; they had lost their precious mothers. One after another, in quick succession, they all died. It was a sad, dark time and it left all of my cousins reeling from grief, all at the same time. There was never going to be a good time, but my bombshell could not have come at a worse time.

There I was at one of the funeral wakes, and a rare opportunity arose where the remainder of my family were all together in one room. I hadn't planned to say anything but, in my already heightened state, with the emotion of the occasion and surrounded by my family that I rarely saw, I found myself desperately needing to connect with my cousins and share my heavy burden. I could feel it bubbling up because of the pent-up grief I had been carrying for years.

Before I had thought it through, I launched into telling one of my cousins about my struggles with Uncle Ivan. He wasn't there and it seemed an opportunity too good to miss. My older cousin, Sally, was aghast, and her sister, who was listening, reeled off a string of angry expletives about Uncle Ivan. Their reaction was absolute shock, and they seemed to side in defence of me which, in the moment, felt good and right.

Unfortunately, the newly revealed news in that room spread like wildfire, and it wasn't long before all the cousins and their adult kids in the room knew too. In that moment, they all believed what I told them. Not one of them questioned what I was saying or considered it untrue. Uncle Ivan was already known for his philandering ways and his arrogant manner. This huge weight of not being believed was lifting off me. I had cousins and family members who accepted what I was saying and didn't reject me; oh, it felt so good!

However, there was a sting in its tail. Out of the blue, my cousin Diana, who was sitting directly in front of me, pulled her chair closer in a challenging manner. "What on earth are you saying, Pippa? Why now, after all these years?" She had anger in her voice and absolutely no grace towards my plight. She launched into an array of questions that she gave no room for any answers. She wasn't really asking questions, she was firing her opinions, thick and fast. She would not let me speak or try to explain my rationale or answer her questions that really weren't questions but felt like accusations.

"Why didn't your mum and dad deal with this years ago?"

"They didn't know the full story back then," I explained, rather poorly. My confidence had been knocked and, by this time, the whole room had whispered my revelations and were all craning their necks to hear this new-found family gossip erupting before their eyes. I had not been brought up to argue and had never had to mercilessly defend myself, especially in public.

Diana had lost her precious Mum and, in sadness looking back, I so wished all the focus had been on the loss of Auntie Kate and nothing had been said. I sensed that was the driving force behind Diana's disdain towards me. I knew, in that moment, that the best thing was to stand up quietly and leave. Admittedly, I'd be walking away from a highly toxic situation that would continue burning long after I had left. I'd dared to open my mouth and try to share my painful story with cousins who I thought would defend me.

In that room on that day, the notion that I was believed was not the issue. In their eyes, I had left it too late...years too late. "What good would it do now?" I questioned myself. "And look at the damage it would cause to Auntie Glenda if she knew! She is in her eighties!"

It's true, I thought; they have a point! But then, as usual, it always felt more important for Auntie Glenda's feelings to be held paramount. Where, oh where were **my** feelings given any credence or acknowledgement? Uncle Ivan had broken me and absolutely no one stopped to recognise the pain he had deposited in me.

Mid-flow of Diana reeling off her opinions over what she thought were new-found revelations, I stood up calmly and walked away, tears rolling down my cheeks, knowing they would never fully understand. Jenny found me broken-hearted in the toilet room, looking in the mirror and hating what I saw: a woman who was hurting, who was now hurting others, and there was no escaping from this pain. From that day, the shared opinion of my cousins was undoubtedly a belief that what I was saying was true, yet each one of them would rather leave it in the past so Auntie Glenda could live in peace. They all clearly refused to dare to imagine how they would have felt had one of their six-year-old daughters found themselves caught, trapped with an uncle who only cared for his own gratification!

After lots of chats and messages, it was clear to me that my cousins loved me, and they were obviously upset by what I had told them. My emotions were certainly in overdrive, and I felt defensive, particularly of the child in me that was so hurt. I knew it was a journey for them, too, and one that we all needed time to adjust to. I often questioned whether they understood the gravity of what I was telling them. From some of their reactions and responses, I realised they could not have fully understood; but who could? Only those who had lived the same trauma could really understand.

Jenny, on the other hand, stood by me from that day and continued to believe what I was saying, understood my heart behind my decision, and only ever wanted whatever would help me to put a stop to my torment and put my past behind me.

During the month that I was weighing up whether or not to report Uncle Ivan to the police, my cousins messaged me several times. I believed they loved me, but they had an inability to be objective and dare to think about what I had really endured.

I had pondered on the idea that the more we allowed and tolerated in our lives, the more ungodliness would be free to abound. We should try to tolerate one another's' weaknesses and flaws and not judge, but a line should be drawn where we must not tolerate serious sin, especially in the form of child abuse. After all, sex with children is against the law. An awful sentence to read, and one I actually just struggled to write, but it was a sentence that was originally said to me that made my insides screw up in utter disdain and objection to its mention.

My reaction pushed me to include it in this book, as this is the reality of what family members are sometimes willing to ignore. Were they really only thinking about Auntie Glenda and her peaceful old age, or were they only thinking about themselves and turning a blind eye so that they did not have to face the real horrors of what sexual abuse entailed?

In a family setting, the hardest thing to do is be willing to expose something that challenges everything. It changes family dynamics, position and relationships, and undoubtedly causes damage along the way. It challenges everyone to take ownership of accepting that the victim is the victim, and the real blame lies fully with the perpetrator.

..........

We had a holiday booked for Tenerife. This was the final week of *the month*. The month where I was thrashing through every conceivable problem and scenario to see if I could go ahead. The most important thing to me was to know that God approved. I could not and would not go ahead without that peace in my heart.

I had Matthew 18:6-8 whirring round my head as it had on and off over the years: *"If anyone causes one of these little ones—those who believe in me—to stumble, it would be better for them to have a large millstone hung around their neck and to be drowned in the depths of the sea. Woe to the world because of the things that cause people to stumble! Such things must come, but woe to the person through whom they come"* The very words of Jesus, clear and defensive of children. Children just like me, who loved Him and trusted in Him, even as a small child.

Although this verse was one that I grew up with and was very familiar with, I always focused on the beginning of the verse where it speaks of His acknowledgement of little children and His love for them, without ever really looking at the gravity of injustice He felt should one of them be hurt. This caused Him to clearly describe the punishment which is fitting and appropriate: drowning in the depths of the sea with a millstone around their neck to keep them there... irredeemable and lost.

If ever there was a verse that spoke of anyone hurting a child and having to pay for it, then this was it. This multifaceted God, who loves us so much that He was willing to send His Son to save us, also wants His little ones to be safe whilst they grow and learn. His love fiercely defends and, as His word says, *"Woe to those who hurt one of my little ones."* But He also reigns in might and power and righteousness, holiness, and justice.

I found it fascinating that all my close Christian friends believed it was right to report Uncle Ivan, yet they based the hub of their being on grace and forgiveness, and generally the people in my life who did not acknowledge Jesus as their Lord, therefore not founding their lives on forgiveness, seemed to struggle with reporting him. It all seemed back-to-front.

As I analysed this, I could see that the ones who honoured God in their lives could not deny the truth even if it was ugly, distasteful and deeply challenging. But the ones who allowed their human feelings to rule their emotions were the ones who would rather brush it under the carpet and choose the easiest life. I could see through this, that God firstly is a Father who completely loves; secondly, that He fiercely defends, and thirdly, would separate, as far as the east is from the west, the offender who hurts and wounds His little ones.

That lesson was enough for me, and I felt that I had the Lord's approval to not only speak out but to report what Uncle Ivan had done. Whatever the outcome, it was Uncle's sin that would cause him to be separated from the loves in his life and pay the price for his crimes. He would be separated from Auntie Glenda and his children, but it was his own utter lack of morality, conscience and betrayal that would put him there.

This holiday was just what I needed, physically, but I felt the emotional weight of the fact that this week was my decision week.

Geoff had a poster on his bedroom wall that I can remember from thirty-five years ago that said, "*7 days without prayer makes one weak!*" Yep, I had one week...and I felt weak. But the contrary became the case as I spent every waking hour praying, seeking God and resting in his presence. As I calmed my thoughts with him, a myriad of new thoughts would come crashing against me throughout the day. *What if I started this thing but couldn't end it? What if I lost my mind? What if Auntie Glenda and Uncle Ivan did end their lives? What if my whole family grew to resent me and only feel disdain towards me? What if Uncle Ivan was so angry at me and he tried to manipulate me into not talking...what would I do?*

I realised I had lived my life pleasing everyone or, at least, trying to. This had to be laid down. I had to wrench out of me the weight that this demanded from me. Approval by God had to be the beginning and end of what really mattered. One by one, I answered each new question, nudging me closer to my decision.

*That was it! Decision made.*

I arrived home on November 10th, 2021. I unpacked my suitcase, made a strong cup of tea, and Ann arrived. She knew what my decision was. Together, we took a deep breath.......and I picked up the phone.

# Chapter Eight
## Two For the Price of One

"Hello. My name is Pippa Rafael. I'd like to report..." *(gasp, gulp)* ... "a crime that happened years ago."

The officer was incredibly kind, and he asked what the nature of the crime was. My heart was pounding, and my mouth instantly dried up. I slowly proceeded to say that my uncle had sexually abused me, starting when I was six years old. As I gave a brief overview, I was told how incredibly brave I was and that I'd definitely made the right decision. The officer told me he would now end the call, but I was to wait an hour, and a specialist officer would call me back for more information. That hour seemed like three hours! Had I just made the biggest mistake of my life? Ann constantly reassured me that I had made the right decision, and this was exactly what should be happening.

The next officer was just as sensitive but had to ascertain things in more detail. After a home visit by the police and a blow-by-blow account of what had happened all those years ago, I was astounded that I'd actually done this. I had made the call and had launched myself on the Criminal Justice journey.

The next day, a wonderful officer called Keith rang me. I will never forget his words to me: "Pippa, you have been fighting this thing all your life. We want you to stop fighting now because we will fight for you!" I cried and cried! Such unbelievably kind words. I was being defended, and by the law of the land! PC Keith could never have known the effects of the depth of care that he conveyed to me and the depth of healing that one sentence began to bring. Someone, in fact a whole system, believed me and were going to take action on my behalf!

Is that not just like Jesus? When we stop the struggle and fighting and give everything to His place of absolute control, power and authority, He defends and fights for us. No one messes with His kids!

In that moment, I felt defended.

Unbeknownst to me while I was processing and deciding whether to report my uncle to the police, I would soon have to make another traumatic, groundbreaking decision.

"So, Pippa," said the detective. "Did you ever have other similar incidents as a child or young person, perpetrated by anyone else?"

I caught my breath, taken aback. I wasn't prepared for that. "Well...erm...yes, but...it's irrelevant. I'm not interested in them as what they did wasn't serious, and my focus is on Uncle Ivan because he caused the majority of the damage." After all, these incidents had happened after my uncle's, and they had been rapidly pushed to the recesses of my mind.

DC Emma extracted the details from a very reluctant, annoyed me, who naively thought that once I'd explained the circumstances and the incidents, she'd just drop them and leave them where they belonged...forgotten.

To my utter disbelief, DC Emma went on to explain that without raising these issues and potentially prosecuting those perpetrators, Uncle Ivan's case may not be able to go ahead as these other incidents might bring this case into question; a court might wonder why I was selective in my decisions which, in turn, could cause questions.

I quickly and happily told her that Clive, the bicycle man who had aggressively pushed me into the corner of his shop, trapping me between his Calor gas heater and his wheelchair, was now dead! He had grabbed me with one hand and pulled me to him, bruising my arms, whilst masturbating with his other. He had belittled, laughed and demanded I listen to his belittling, forcing me to look at the porn strewn across his floor. He had then released me and commanded me to clean him and the floor. Thank goodness he was dead and that I did not have to repeat this to a string of important, scrutinising people.

Which then left a church elder, who I felt had been more inappropriate than criminal. Fortunately, we skimmed past that one...for now, anyway.

Finally, there was Jerry. Now, *his* actions *were* damaging and the repercussions longer lasting. Still not as serious, in my eyes, but DC Emma did not agree.

Here, I was being told that in the next couple of days, I would be going to the police station to be interviewed about Uncle Ivan, but also that I would be getting a call from another police force who would require me to visit their station and go through exactly the same process concerning Jerry.

..........

I arrived with Ann at the police station to be interviewed about Uncle Ivan formally, by doing my ABE (Achieving Best Evidence) interview.

I had made notes beforehand but, by the time I went in, the paper was totally crumpled and curled up as my nerves were shot through the roof. My fingers had fiddled with the papers till they were gnarled and looked more like relics!

This was it...the police interview! I had to get this right. I must remember every detail. I couldn't forget anything. The pressure felt immense.

One of my worries was that I would not be able to remember enough because some of my memories are fractured and incomplete. I can remember the start of most of Uncle Ivan's 'sessions' but some of those memories vanish in the middle and I often have no recollection of the endings. I remember being in one place but, in the next moment, I'm in another room, completely skipping the in-between bit.

Then there are those times that are as clear as yesterday; I remember the clothes I was wearing, and the surroundings, and other details that are firmly logged in my memory. All those things made me feel my story had no real substance or consistency.

Trauma has such an effect on the mind that God, in His mercy, knew how to form our brain so we could, in that moment, protect ourselves. God never intended us to be hurt, threatened or damaged, but He set in motion a mechanism, should that be the case. The brain switches its response, and, during the moment of perceived fear, the brain locks itself into the self-protection of freeze, flight and fight and other responses. This is not a choice or decision; therefore, we have no control over it. As children, we have no strength and no capability or capacity to offset the power imbalance that is thrust upon us during abuse.

The police made it incredibly clear that even if there are parts of information missing, what mattered was that the truth was told, regardless of how small or fragmented the memories were. They described it as a jigsaw: each bit of detail mattered, no matter how small or confused, and each part was important in piecing together the full picture.

I was seated in a fresh, bright room that had sofas and an intrusive-looking eye in the corner, recording every movement and word. As another detective sat in the other room listening, recording, and working out additional questions, DC Emma sat herself down calmly with a paper full of questions and enquiries, poised and ready to begin. It felt like a parallel universe; what we were involved in didn't seem like real life and was certainly like nothing I had experienced before.

I launched into my story, which was what DC Emma had asked me to do. "Just say your name and age and start at the beginning!"

Unbelievably, it all came out synchronised and in order, and I believe I managed to include everything, all in chronological order. As always, the Lord went before me and He touched my speech and mind with clarity, something I rarely have in stressful situations, which is quite natural when going through or reliving trauma.

Although it flowed, I was deeply embarrassed as I had great difficulty saying some of the things that happened. "Oh, not the P-word!" Yep, I had to say it: "*Penis!*" One of my biggest worries was how I was going to describe things. All the correct words felt like wrong words. '*Down there*' is not good enough. The police not only wanted every correct word, but they also wanted every bad word too (especially swearing), and anything that described the moment and the conduct of the perpetrator. Suddenly, every word counted, and Uncle Ivan would have to give an account for what he had said and done. The police could make no mistakes in understanding exactly what had taken place. Somehow it felt right, though. If there was ever a time that I could say everything, it was now.

My mum and dad had drilled into us that we needed to keep our mouths pure. As a child, I found it hilarious that she absolutely stood by her principles, but when she had opportunity to say, 'grass sod', she said it with gusto, and it wasn't for any other reason than her rebellious streak being able to say the word '*sod*'!

After two-and-a-half hours in the police interview room, I'd finished my recollections of the horrendous incidents. As I was rounding up, the other detective came in and asked several more intrusive questions, by which time I had lost my shyness and was able to answer promptly. In that moment, I so wanted them to know what Uncle Ivan had done, and then that was it. They both seemed really happy with the interview and said they had everything they needed.

I went to stand, but my legs were weak. I had taken my mum's handkerchief, which was now sodden as I'd cried quietly throughout the whole interview and my nose had run profusely. Pulling my wobbly, sniffly self together, I was escorted out of the building with Ann, and I looked at her, amazed that we had actually done it! After all these years, we had got there!

*I'd reported him!*

As I opened the car door to get in, blood drained from my legs and I instantly felt weak, falling to the floor and hitting the concrete. It had been incredibly emotional, and my anxiety levels had been through the roof. The fresh air and the enormity of what I'd just done had hit me.

..........

Two weeks later, it was time for round two: the ABE interview to unpack the incidents concerning Jerry. Reluctantly, I arrived at the police station, this time of a different Police force. So, a different detective constable was running my case, and another officer was in the other room, recording and writing new questions whenever he felt clarification or more information was needed.

His questions were tough and pushed me further than I expected my recall to stretch. I couldn't see the importance of such graphic questioning at the time, but realised further down the track how important it was to establish the exact gravity of the abuse in order to come to the right charging decision. DC Hannah led the interview and my case against Jerry. She was calm and clear, and led me through the process with as much ease as possible. It was the first time I had actually realised how what I unpacked sounded like to other people. It sounded serious and criminal. Pushing it into the recesses of my mind all those years ago certainly protected my mind but hiding it hadn't dealt with it or stopped its effects on me.

Jerry, my precious friend's husband who was in his twenties when I was eleven years old, had taken every advantage of my vulnerability. I had been happily and excitedly helping my church friend with the care of her children. I'd loved babies since I was very young. Here was my chance, in church, to play and spend time with her little ones. She valued the help, and I loved our times together. I started to stay over, and, after a few visits, Jerry lurked round every corner, out of sight waiting for me to pass by, and singled me out. He masturbated repeatedly whilst I was made to stand and watch him, rigid to the spot in fear. Fear of the present and fear of what might happen next; how was I to know what would follow? Uncle Ivan had secured that response. Jerry would lie on me in bed and breathe heavily into my face, whilst I wrapped myself up in tightly in my quilt in desperation to stay untouched by him. He'd already insisted he watched me in the bath and had instructed me on how to wash. I was humiliated and deeply distressed.

Things escalated to him forcefully and aggressively assaulting me and digitally penetrating me. The questions during the interview were brutal, and I squirmed in my chair as the male officer from the other room came through, asking for more detail.

It had taken forty-eight years to report Uncle Ivan, so how did this officer think he was going to get more out of me after only two weeks of warning that I would be questioned on this!

Finally, it was all complete and my second interview was done!

## Chapter Nine
# Waiting

"So, what happens next?"

This was one of the hardest parts to deal with: the waiting. What was I waiting for? I didn't really know. I didn't know what I should be doing, or not doing, or how or what I should be feeling.

It was at this stage that I was introduced to Julie by the police. She was my ISVA (Independent Sexual Violence Adviser), and it was her job to advocate between myself and the police, keeping me updated on where the investigation and progressing case was at. She was there to explaining the whole process and help me with the difficulties and challenges that arise from such a journey. She also kept my officer informed on how I was doing and coping with the whole thing. Not a small task for Julie, as it handled the most sensitive subject of rape and sexual abuse, and she had to manoeuvre around my ever-changing emotions. "And normal emotions they are, given this abnormal situation," was her mantra. Without her, I could not have survived the criminal justice process and my own fears and questioning that drove me mad on a daily basis...ok, admittedly, an hourly basis.

Julie's was the weekly phone call that I waited for eagerly to give some perspective to the process. She had a great raucous laugh and wit that whipped me out of my spiralling woes, more often than not. She became an integral part of my journey as she sat in her window during our phone calls, complaining about her poor Wi-Fi connection. She knew the road ahead was long and uncertain, and it was her job to talk to me with the greatest optimism whilst always delivering the reality that I may not receive what I set out to achieve... a conviction! Furthermore, two convictions!

During this time, I seemed to lose my sense of humour. Everything became so serious to me, and nothing seemed funny anymore. I began to feel incredibly isolated. Who could understand such a complex emotionally charged process unless they'd been through it? What did a police investigation even entail? I had no idea.

Thank goodness Julie was able to lead me through this. She was 'in the know' and she had walked a myriad of men, women and children through the same process. All different, with a unique set of circumstances surrounding them, and each one unique in the details of their abuse. No one story is exactly the same, yet they all have a commonality that requires those around them to handle them with care.

There were a few people around me saying, "Oh well, there's nothing you can do now; it's in the hands of the police, just let them do their job. Don't think about it."

"Oh boy! Don't think about it! Are they nuts?" I'm a really tolerant person, but this made me want to knock their teeth out. This was my life at its most vulnerable. This was everything laid bare, and this was me, the wounded little girl who would be questioned, and retraumatised, all whilst being a wife, a mum, a friend and, on top of that, having a hefty responsibility to nurture the additional children I had in my care.

How would they find any evidence, let alone enough? Who on earth would be interviewed? What would be unearthed? More victims? More secrets? And, unbelievably, there were two lots of investigations running right alongside each other.

This was no 200-metre sprint; it was a cross country run with the worst terrain. It needed guts and gritted teeth, and I increasingly felt I didn't have what it took....and all the while, people were saying, "Try not to think about it!"

The Detective Constable leading my case was Danny Gallucci. He was the sort of cop that made you stand to attention and made you feel like you absolutely must make sure everything you said was correct. I often found myself rambling, through nerves. Goodness knows what he thought of me! He was a very black-and-white type of person and said things with no frills...no mincing his words or wasting them. He did not show much emotion at first, which put me slightly on edge. It took some time to adapt to his approach, but it wasn't long before I learnt to appreciate his total dependability on getting the job done thoroughly, leaving no stone unturned.

Whilst waiting, I had built myself up to the point where I was terrified that it would all pass away in a puff of smoke and be over because there was not enough evidence. I was eating and breathing this, awake and whilst dreaming. This waiting for the next step was all-consuming. I'd told them everything, so why weren't the police arresting him or at least taking him in for questioning?

The idea of that was a huge thing, in itself. How would that look to people? Auntie and Uncle, both in their eighties and, as I had seen on 'Law and Order UK', the police go first thing in the morning to catch them at home and off-guard.

That thought was too surreal! My respectable Auntie Glenda and Uncle Ivan in their PJs! Uncle sitting reading the paper; Auntie flicking through Facebook whilst eating their seeded toasted batch bread smothered in jam, oblivious to the scheduled order the police were silently positioning themselves in, outside the property. Plain clothes officers going in first and then probably a group of uniformed officers at the front and back of the property. Maybe a couple of cars and a van! I imagined the neighbours pulling back the curtains, peeping through the blinds, on their very respectable, immaculate street.

This was for real! But when would it happen?

At this stage, I was full of anxiety, reliving every detail of the abuse that Uncle had put me through. Each time I did it, I felt the need to underestimate and minimise the whole thing, all the time saying to myself, "There are so many worse things that happen!" I was in a strange cycle of questioning the seriousness of the offences and minimising them, and other times trying to convince myself that they were serious, and the arrest was something that had to happen.

Was what happened so bad? I'd start at the beginning of the abuse and walk myself through each incident, questioning and grading each one, only to land at the end and feel the need to start all over again from the beginning just in case I got it wrong. It was my brain trying to process what happened but also trying to give credibility to what I'd said and make sure, in my head, that I had given an accurate representation of the events.

I'd always had a tendency to minimise the incidents and, even now, I still have to guard myself against it. However, during this time, it was overwhelmingly intense, and I could just not shake it for a few months.

However, the Crown Prosecution Service are very clear on the laws concerning sexual offences. I learnt, as time progressed, that regardless of what I thought was acceptable / not too bad / could be worse, if there was a law or legislation against it, irrespective of my opinion, it is wrong, and a prosecution could be made. What I had told the police in detail, they had called 'rape' and 'serious sexual assault'. This made me do the deepest gulp, but I could not argue as it wasn't me who made the rules.

It had taken three months for the four police forces to communicate and decide who was taking on the case through the investigation and beyond. It had finally rested with the Scottish Police as they said the second lot of abuse was carried out in Scotland. In addition, Uncle Ivan and Auntie Glenda were now living there and had done since it happened in their house forty years previously.

So that was when DC Danny Gallucci had become involved. He had rung me one Wednesday morning, and my heart had pounded from the onset.

"Pippa, I'm running your case. I need names, addresses and dates of birth of anyone at all who might know anything. Anyone, from the moment it happened to now. Anyone who you think would be willing to talk to the police and give us a statement to add their piece of the jigsaw."

I, in my forward thinking, had already got my list prepared. During the month I took to decide whether this was possible, I had wracked my brain to remember all the incidents through the years, and snippets of information I'd leaked out or told in some effort to get help or just be heard. I was surprised that I had manage to rack up quite a list.

There was Brett, the Youth Leader, who I told at fourteen years of age, albeit doing nothing except giving me a pat on the shoulder. Matt, my best friend, to whom I rather chaotically spilled out my disclosure whilst he listened in disbelief. My friend Anna, to whom I fumbled a few words at around nineteen years of age. My cousins Jenny and Claire, who were present on the holiday when the dreadful abuse happened.

I also gave Auntie Glenda's address and name which, of course, was Uncle Ivan's address too, but it was with such deep sadness that I wrote it, as my sense of betrayal towards her felt overwhelming.

My brother Joey, my cousins' names, my GP and a minister. Unfortunately, my old counsellor couldn't be used as he had passed away. That was a source of disappointment for the police as he could have held some vital information which was never retrieved, despite a thorough search for it.

DC Gallucci seemed pleased with my list, and I was very pleased that I had done my homework…even finding phone numbers and addresses of people I hadn't seen for decades. DC Gallucci took these and then, from my ABE Interview, he formed as many questions as he could to create a structured, suspect police interview, ready to confront Uncle Ivan head-on in an intense few hours of questioning.

Between giving my evidence and Uncle Ivan being apprehended, I had grown very nervous as there was something I hadn't told them, and I started to worry that I would be in trouble if they found out at later date. My deep, troubled worry was the fact that I still had the phone call - the one where I had recorded my conversation with Uncle Ivan about his reasons for doing what he did to me, and my anxieties and difficulties that came from that abuse.

Geoff told me I couldn't withhold it, and that it could be vital evidence. "But how could it?" I retorted. "I recorded it without his knowledge or permission!"

Needless to say, Geoff won. I was so nervous that I had been withholding information, and believed I'd be in a lot of trouble because of it, but I relented and rang DC Gallucci and told him. He reassured me by saying I had absolutely done the right thing by telling him, and he had it in its possession fifteen minutes later, saying, "Let's see what we can do with this!" The decision had been made, much to my relief.

Christmas 2021 was almost unbearable. On the eve of Christmas Eve, the police rang to inform me that if they were to get the chance, they would be going to Uncle Ivan's on Christmas Eve! I was sent into a spin.

I heard nothing! The day passed, and Christmas Eve came and went, and I still had no idea if Uncle Ivan had been arrested or not. The pit of my stomach was so sick. Maybe the prawns in there that I'd swallowed from my Christmas starter were all flipping over…they certainly felt alive! How could I enjoy my Christmas dinner when he was possibly being plucked from his home on the happiest day of the year? Maybe, while I was eating Christmas dinner, he was locked in a cell: desperate, terrified and alone. I felt sick! So sick!

I tried to smile, laugh, and make Christmas happy for everyone, but I was utterly traumatised internally. My face went numb, and my extremities sent the blood away to maintain the survival of my brain and major organs. Apparently, this is what can happen when someone is in severe shock and suffering trauma. I was suffering silently, as usual.

This was scary on every level for me. I was totally anguished over the uncertainty and dread of what was about to happen, fearful of a backlash from Auntie, and terrified of Uncle Ivan's reaction. However, I got the distinct impression that no one else around me had a clue about what was in my head; to all intents and purposes, they were all too busy enjoying Christmas. It was reminiscent of when I was fourteen and enduring Uncle Ivan's assaults whilst everyone around me was laughing and chatting, utterly oblivious to what was happening under their noses.

New Year's Eve came and went, and I heard nothing.

# Chapter Ten
## A Duo of Arrests

As the new year came and fireworks shot into the sky, I couldn't help but gasp at the thought of what the year ahead held. Everyone around me seemed to have forgotten about the investigations. As for me, my life was now on hold. The pause button had been firmly pressed down and I could not see the light at the end of the tunnel. I felt empty and couldn't stop myself from spiralling down and reaching for another drink once the dinner pots had been washed and everyone had disbanded for the evening. Well, it passed another evening and pushed me into the next day.

I felt such guilt as I knew I was displeasing the Lord, despite entering a new phase of my understanding of Him. I was always led to believe that my actions and behaviours needed to be determined by God's approval or lack of I was starting to understand the heart of the Father...*my* Father. His heart hurt when my heart hurt; His understanding of my frailty was complete. He LOVES me, regardless of my weaknesses. He is eager, desperate, in fact, reaching with His hand permanently outstretched towards me. He doesn't just look at my ungodly coping mechanisms and judge them; He lovingly gazed beyond that. He saw the hurt and floundering child that was lost in the waiting-for-protection and desperation to feel a sense of safety inside. Jesus was my bedrock, yet I kept letting go of His hand! No wonder I felt lost.

Waiting for something that will change the trajectory of your life when you have no idea of the course it will take, is not only deeply unsettling but also disturbing. My insecurities were screaming at me, and I had no idea how to calm them. Was I the only one who felt like I was holding my breath?

Julie's weekly afternoon calls scraped me from one week to the next. They always started, "It's only Julie," so Geoff and I called her 'Only Julie' affectionately for the next three years.

Julie knew the cost of such a road. Less than one percent of victims manage to successfully complete this journey. Many of her clients, who start the journey, quit at various stages, finding it all too much for a variety of reasons. Some, as Julie put it, 'took to their beds'. They stopped washing and dressing, and just hid themselves away, their mental health taking a real battering. Julie worked so hard to keep her clients on track...me being one of them.

"But Julie, nothing is happening!" I said, repeatedly. "Are they even doing anything?"

"It's all in hand, and yes, they are working hard at getting everything in place, Pippa."

Julie had worked with DC Gallucci before and knew his style of policing. She assured me that he was getting on with the case, regardless of what felt like a lack of movement and minimal communication from him.

February 3$^{rd}$ arrived, and, to my utter shock and astonishment, I received an email at 08:10. It was from DC Gallucci.

*Pippa, this is just to let you know, we are going to speak to Ivan first thing this morning. I will update you later.*

There it was: the notification I had waited and longed for! I stood up and paced around and told Geoff, who looked poised with expectation, his eyes widened. We both repeated over and over, "This is it!"

My brain went into overdrive. "Oh, poor Auntie Glenda...it's her birthday!" How utterly awful! I'd already gone through every scenario of the series of events following the arrival of the detectives and police officers crossing her threshold, but... today of all days, her birthday! She probably had not even opened her cards...and what if Uncle Ivan hadn't even written it yet! Horrendous!

I put my head in my hands and sobbed for her. The day stood still, and I couldn't stop moving. Neither could my mouth. I repeated over and over, "Oh Jesus, oh Jesus, oh Jesus!"

I needed Him. I meant it; I needed Him to hold me and calm my nerves, I needed the police to arrest Uncle Ivan, but I also needed Auntie to be ok. But how could she be? Who on earth would be? The police cannot even tell the wife what's happening without the accused's permission, and that was unlikely as he was not going to want them saying why they were there in front of Auntie. What on earth would they even be arresting him on? I nervously started a string of chores but couldn't finish any of them. Coffee! That was what I needed! Strong coffee and a giant piece of Rocky Road cake from a local café.

Eventually, I sat at a poorly wiped table in Delfie and Dine, checking my phone for the umpteenth time and stared at all the ladies that lunch, gossiping about life... and then...my phone rang! I jumped out of my skin, knocking over my tea, which filled the saucer mercilessly.

Oh boy! *Caller withheld!* I jumped to my feet and answered, sheepishly. DC Gallucci spoke. "Pippa, we have him."

"Really?"

He went on to say that they were preparing to start the interview, and he would update me once that had happened. I was amazed, grateful and absolutely terrified all in one go. My teeth banged together just like they did all those years ago because of Uncle Ivan.

It wasn't until the following day that DC Gallucci rang to tell me how the interview had gone, and I could barely take it all in.

Uncle Ivan had been arrested for rape and sexual abuse. It hit me between the eyes. I expected it to be toned down and not so blatant, but I guess how much softer can something like that be said?

DC Gallucci went on to say that Uncle Ivan had denied everything; in fact, it was what is called a 'no comment' interview. Apart from a statement he made when he first arrived ("I'm NOT GUILTY of any sexual crime!"), he stuck to his guns and wouldn't speak. The police went from every angle and asked him every question possible, but he would not relent. Why was I not surprised? Although in my heart of hearts I had hoped, in a fairytale world, that he would admit his guilt and acknowledge the pain that he had put me through, in my more realistic moments, I hadn't expected him to own up to anything. He always gave an air of believing that he was above everything – obviously, even the law.

DC Gallucci flabbergasted me with his next bit of information. The police had extracted Uncle Ivan's voice from the phone call and had played it to him, there and then. "Is this your voice, Ivan?"

Uncle Ivan had replied immediately and said, "Yes, yes, it is." This was just what DC Gallucci had wanted to hear.

Much to my horror, he explained that he had gone on to play the full phone call. By this point, my eyes were tightly shut, and I couldn't believe it had been played to him this early on. *Oh, Uncle Ivan will be so very angry with me! He now knows that I recorded it!* I guess, when was a good or right time to play it, but during the interview!

Uncle Ivan had refused to admit that the subject matter was sexual, never mind sexual abuse. Admittedly, during the phone call, neither of us had mentioned a private body part or what was done to either of our bodies. It was all about the aftereffects, my feelings and asking him about his feelings...with one exception. During the phone call, Uncle Ivan had mentioned that I had rubbed the hairs on his legs as a six-year-old and that I'd gone too high.

DC Gallucci had questioned me about that when he had first listened to the recording. I had been fuming! That was NOT TRUE, I did NOT go too high! "NO, NO, that's NOT true!" I had blurted out in annoyance to DC Gallucci. "That's not fair at all. I might have only been six, but I would never have gone too high, touching his private parts!" He had accepted what I'd said, and I had calmed down. He had explained that he had needed to ask because Uncle Ivan had said it on the recording. I guess he had to be able to put up a defence...anyone does, who is accused of something.

He was released on bail whilst a full investigation into all the allegations was undertaken. This must have been the worst birthday that Auntie Glenda had ever had. As much as I had wanted this to happen, the fact that it *had* happened made me feel dreadful, sick and totally responsible. Well now, that was it; Auntie Glenda would finally know why I had withdrawn all those months ago, and I hoped she would understand that I'd had no choice.

DC Gallucci spent the next few months finding evidence and piecing it together to hopefully bring the case to a place where it met the 'threshold'. Only when the Sergeant and Inspector agreed that there was enough evidence and they believed there's a good chance of prosecution, the case could be handed over to the CPS (Crime Prosecution Service).

When the news I had been waiting for finally arrived, I could hardly believe it! It had passed the test and DC Gallucci was thrilled to say that he'd handed it over to the CPS.

"So, is that it then? Will he be prosecuted?" I was excited, for a moment and, in that moment, all the waiting felt worth it.

"No, Pippa. It doesn't work like that. The CPS will now examine the case and ask more questions. Then, if they feel they can prosecute, they will then make the charging decision. The allegations must be formally charged, and a CPS lawyer must work through every sexual act and surrounding circumstances to decide by law what is, in fact, a crime, and what category it falls under."

Talk about thorough! Julie helped me understand. "We are talking about serious crimes against a child, and we are also talking about a man's freedom. The evidence must be clear to be able to apply the law.

June 16th came, and DC Gallucci rang me while I was on holiday. I could barely answer the call as I was so nervous that there may be a problem. I braced myself for him to say, "I'm sorry, Pippa, but the case has been dropped."

On the contrary, I couldn't believe my ears! The CPS had taken on the case, and they were going to bring a prosecution case against Uncle Ivan! They had also made their charging decisions. DC Gallucci sent them to me. I was stunned as I read them.

There were nine charges in all. DC Gallucci was clearly happy with the great result and the number of charges.

Uncle Ivan, on the other hand, was shocked at how many there were. "How could he be shocked?" I wondered. As I had gone through my continuous loop of scrutinising what he had done to me, I had realised that there were lots of things that were very definitely wrong. Had he forgotten them? How on earth could he? They'd changed my life irrevocably. Or maybe he just did not want to admit it.

Julie repeatedly reminded me that paedophiles continually excuse their behaviour to themselves, and relentlessly live in denial and a constant mindset that says, 'I'm innocent' and shift the blame somewhere else.

I learnt that the charges don't count how many times an incident happened but are based on different categories, and there could be several repeated acts under one category. This list of chargers did not show the exact crime, but that was to become clear further along the journey. All I knew was that I was repeatedly being told by Julie and DC Gallucci that these were very serious sexual crimes and must not be minimised.

Exactly a week after Uncle Ivan had been arrested, Jerry was also arrested! The officer for this case had a similar response to Uncle Ivan's, during the interview. Jerry also insisted that he wasn't guilty and would not acknowledge anything at all. Apparently, this is not unusual in a lot of suspect interviews with accused paedophiles. He said that not only had he never met me, but that he'd never even heard of me. DC Hannah interviewed him at length. She went from every angle and Jerry's best defence at that time was to say he had suffered amnesia around the time of the allegations. I couldn't believe it!

"Surely that's not a defence!" I said to the officer.

Jerry had said he could not possibly be held responsible as he had no memory of what had happened, but DC Hannah reassured me that amnesia isn't necessarily a good defence as it does not prove the crime wasn't committed, whether remembered or not.

Jerry was released on bail and, yet again, I felt nervous…very nervous. To add to my existing battle of trying to navigate Uncle Ivan's criminal proceedings, I now had to do the same for Jerry's. I knew Uncle Ivan, which gave a little comfort, but I had no idea of Jerry's character and how he would react to being put under this scrutiny and pressure. I felt unsafe and found myself looking over my shoulder wherever I went. I had no idea what he looked like now, forty years later.

## Chapter Eleven
## Layer Upon Layer

Out of the blue, along came Dan and Sophia back into our lives after many years. The last time Geoff and I had seen them, we all had mullets (apart from Dan, who always had a very suave haircut and what my mum called a very tidy shirt). Unbelievably, he still had the same attire! Both still slim, not like us who had thickened round the middle and our tidy shirts were now roomy and what my mother would have described as "unkempt".

They were the new pastors at *The River* church. We had been looking for some time for a church closer to home, although I felt nervous and unsure of the commitment. I was in a very vulnerable position, scared and defensive. I felt I had to keep my walls up and not allow anyone else to know what was going on in my life. There was no way I was going to open up to them and blight another relationship, which was how I believed I affected all my relationships.

I had Ann and Rob, who knew everything, and I was really nervous to once again be honest about the horrendous circumstances I found myself in with more people, especially a new church full.

Unbeknown to me, Sophia was a councillor, and unbeknown to her I had a generous, bucket-load of trauma. A friend who could not be my counsellor but understood me was God given. She didn't have the responsibility of weekly sessions, but I definitely gave her the responsibility of chai tea making! On walking our circuits of the block during Covid, we repeatedly bumped into them. We tried not to jump to conclusions that it was part of God's plan, but we certainly could not help but wonder.

Not only did we have a lovely connection from a previous church (Goldlang church), but what I needed at that time, they had. They too, in return, needed more friends as they were coming through Covid times whilst joining and leading a new church in a new area.

They arrived in our lives at just the right time to add to the support Rob and Ann already gave me. 'Team Pippa', as we all started calling it, was birthed. I found myself allowing them into my journey and, as the criminal justice process was progressing, I needed daily support as things were hotting up and my emotions were as wild as a herd of antelope fleeing from a lion. I was all over the place, up and down, and felt as if my life was coming to an end. "Is it worth it?" I asked myself.

The CPS got in touch, and I could not believe it. They had taken Jerry's case on. Simeon, the Prosecutor, said that they viewed Jerry's offences as serious and that they had categorised them. He explained that Jerry had been sent his letter and had been charged with seven offences.

These offences were listed, detailing exactly what the sexual acts were…not like Uncle Ivan's, which were listed as sexual assaults and rape, without describing the acts. Jerry's were more graphic in their charging description.

I found this really difficult. Seeing them all written in black and white, I felt dirty and embarrassed. I could not believe that the two of them were being prosecuted for sixteen offences committed against me in total!

I could not show my kids and neither did I want Geoff to see. The shame I thought I'd dealt with still had another layer. I still feared exposure and powerlessness. It felt so strong. Exposure of what? I was not guilty of what happened to me but neither did I feel completely innocent. The very fact I had been involved, and part of Jerry's games, made me hold a view that his dirt and something of him was left on me - something immoral and unworthy. This was also how I felt about Uncle Ivan.

Shame felt like a good thing to me as it kept me in my place. I felt like I had to punish myself. It felt good, and anyway it was only in my internal monologue and not hurting anyone else. At this time it felt right to me.

People often think that a session or two of counselling, a session of prayer or maybe just the passage of time deals with shame. However, sexual trauma has an insidious effect, and it can appear to be gone but then raises its head when it's least expected. It is part of a cycle of unseen perception. Shame creeps around, hiding. It doesn't parade itself. In fact, it is quite shy and subtle in its ways. A sense of unworthiness hangs around with guilt and, together, they keep changing hands with each other, always ready to step up when I was faced with any sense of suffering that I felt I had caused.

I imagined that Uncle Ivan was probably suffering beyond belief and Jerry was most certainly at his wits end with anguish. So surely, I should be suffering too. I could not let myself off the hook and even wrongly thought that I *shouldn't*.

No amount of Ann or Sophia or anyone telling me that both men were in this mess because of what *they* had done made any difference or impact on me. It was like I had an emotional shield that it bounced off. I was not ready to let go of what I thought was my guilt and my shame in putting both men through this process - this voyage of vileness.

Sometimes I stopped and was brutal with myself, totally ignoring everyone else's opinions. *Did Uncle Ivan and Jerry deserve this? Was their suffering justified?* In honesty, I couldn't answer this...but the law had an answer...a very clear answer in the form of sixteen charges! I had to allow it to speak. I had no choice.

Shame primarily drives us into hiding. It encourages us to go into hiding from ourselves, hiding from others and, ultimately, from God. Shame brings a person into a life of isolation, and any positive self-image at all is sabotaged and eventually replaced. Initially, this place will feel safe and secure but it's not a happy or comfortable place. Jesus' heart for us is always, without exception, to lead us to His Father, who takes huge delight in helping His children grow into His very own image. Shame cannot hold hands with God. It has no option but to partner with Satan; thus, our involvement identifies with the one with whom we are partnering. To make shame a shelter in one's life will fundamentally and ultimately cause that person to lose themselves.

I was sick of hearing the 'onion' analogy of layers: layers of things needing to be dealt with, all causing tears, all relentless and never-ending. I prefer to imagine the Earth and its layers. Different thicknesses, pressures, structures, atmospheres, and temperatures. But the fundamental difference is that there's a clearly defined core, a centre that can be reached. I needed constant reminders of the truth. He is the way, the truth and the life...and I needed Him to work through my layers to reach and heal my core.

Truth cannot be overridden or dissolved. It stands and remains. I knew full well that because I belonged to Jesus, I was not forever lost in this onion mentality, but rather in the Earth mentality; there was a centre, and my Father would take me through all the layers to renew my mind and set me free, even freeing me from shame and guilt.

He had given me a scripture years ago as I, at fifteen years old, laid in my hospital bed, struggling with another critical asthma attack. He spoke clearly and I scrambled through my wires to grab my Bible.

Isaiah 54:4 read: *You will forget the shame of your youth*. I knew back then this had been imprinted on my heart and that one day I would be finally free from it.

This was something that had to be fought for, and still needs to be, but to have a promise is an anchor. I'm learning never to despise the anchors of promise from God, even if they seem delayed or unattainable. These promises hold you, even when you are battered; you cannot be washed away or destroyed, because someone greater holds you firm. Jesus had to endure humiliation and nakedness, and He was vulnerable. Vulnerable to the nails that held Him. He had nowhere to turn and as He shouted, *"My God, my God, why have you forsaken me?"* He had, in that moment, no protection...and He was a spectacle for whoever stood and looked upon His shame.

That is how sexual abuse makes you feel. You see what others don't see about yourself and feel what others don't feel about you. But Jesus willingly hung there. He allowed shame to become a spectacle in full view of everyone. He exposed it and bore it so you and I could be free from our private shame and pain, but Jesus appeared to be peeling off my layers of shame in stages...and it was part of an ongoing process for me.

## Chapter Twelve
### Rizla Paper

As a child I had lost so much, and I was too busy protecting myself in survival mode to notice. I had survived my uncle's first spree of assaults, as well as the other two people, only to feel that I couldn't deal with it, so I didn't, and just pushed it away from me.

It was only as time passed that I began to realise something was lost. I had lost the joy and wonder of a child's early life that gives everything that curious and exciting feel; being able to explore life without fear or inhibition...in other words, to experience childhood.

The loss of those healthy early years had left a chasm and a missing link. This link was something that I was only just beginning to realise was missing. Grieving for something I never had has been a hard concept to understand. When a child isn't rescued from sexual abuse, there grows a sense in your soul of being orphaned and subsequently left without direction.

The adult protects, defends and brings solutions to children's lives but, in my life, although my parents were in no way guilty of abandoning me, neither did they realise that I desperately needed their protection, which is often the case in a family. No one sees what is happening, as the abuser has learnt to be skilled at manipulation and flying under the radar. I had the dearest dad who adored me, but without his intervention when I needed it above anything else, I was left with my soul floundering and feeling abandoned.

Sometimes, I don't know what to do with myself or how to feel but, more than that, I cannot even identify what is wrong. This comes from a heart that felt abandoned and had to fight for its own survival and had rooted a grief and loss in my soul. I knew this was something that needed healing, and I had begun to recognise it. This was the first step.

I started to forget about Jerry and that court process as Uncle Ivan's plea hearing rapidly approached. It was to be at the High Court Justiciary in Scotland, just before Christmas. At least I would know how he intended to plead in time for Christmas, and I would be able to relax a little. Well, that was, again, most people's idea of how I should be feeling. Sometimes, I could not help but think that people wanted the process to be easier for me for their own benefit, then they would be off the hook and didn't have to think or worry about it. Without them realising, it became about them and not me.

I was, in fact, a mess and couldn't help but down copious amounts of alcohol to just numb things for a few hours. One night, I stumbled round to Dan and Sophia's, flopping down on their kitchen floor. I just sobbed and felt wretched. It all felt so unfair; all just too much.

How was I going to stand against Uncle Ivan? The age-old feelings of total inadequacy and feeling the victim encircled me. I hated that, but the truth was that if there was a hierarchy, then I felt like I was at the bottom. He called the shots; it was in his hands whether he admitted his guilt or decided to fight to the bitter end and pick me apart, bit by bit. He would do it subtly because he knew I was only a child when it happened, maybe questioning the validity of my memories and how clear they could be. I had never won, back then, so how on earth did I think I could win now? He had the intelligence and charm, and I felt like a snivelling, unbalanced woman, only just managing to survive each day.

Sophia sat with me into the night listening to my contemptible self-loathing and grief. She did not share my view of myself, but she could see my pain and, rather than try to pull me out of it, she gave it acknowledgement and her agreement that this was astronomically difficult. Always, without fail, she said how well I was doing.

It always reduced me to tears as I looked back on the night, as it reminded me of Jesus. He sits with us, alongside us. He nurses our wounded hearts and heals us with his love and mercy, He is so slow to be angry and he abounds in love.

Oh, I needed mercy, but I felt like I needed punishment. I was so angry at myself. But now, more than ever, I needed God's mercy. He richly, abundantly, and without measure, poured it over and over again into my heart. These pockets of waves came over me, often out of the blue, when I least expected them. The lifeline that Christ throws to us always has Him at one end. He can see us suffocating, questioning and almost drowning, but He is ALWAYS there. In His mercy, absolutely nothing could sever our connection.

From being a young child, and even during the abuse, my Heavenly Father kept touching my heart and I woud sing this song to Him. In that moment, for a moment, the pain, grief and loss would be replaced by His unfailing love, and I felt it tangibly.

*Draw me close to You*
*Never let me go*
*I lay it all down again*
*To hear You say that I'm Your friend*
*You are my desire*

*No one else will do*
*'Cause nothing else can take Your place*
*To feel the warmth of Your embrace*
*Help me find the way*
*Bring me back to You*

*You're all I want*
*You're all I've ever needed*
*You're all I want*
*Help me know You are near.*

*(1994 Mercy/Vineyard Publishing*
*Admin by Vineyard Music USA)*

The desperate times were so desperate, but the pockets of awareness of His love were so precious.

Julie was ringing regularly, and she had increased her calls to prepare me for court and also the worst, should it happen. "Usually, Pippa, men like Uncle Ivan plead not guilty." She had seen this so often: perpetrators with no remorse and not even a flicker of acknowledgement on their faces. Sin does that! When anyone repeatedly and relentlessly goes on to do something against God's laws and, in this case, the laws of the land concerning children, their hearts harden, and deception, denial and death creeps in. Their whole world view changes so they live in their own elevated approval whilst being in total denial of the devastation and damage they leave in their victims' lives.

I did not have to attend the plea hearing, but DC Gallucci rang me soon after. Uncle Ivan had, indeed, pleaded *'not guilty'* and a trial date had been set for June 14th!

Six months away! Another long wait! As much as I had realised that this was part and parcel of the tedious journey of the criminal justice process, each block of time was another trial in itself. I was facing more months of dealing with all these erratic emotions.

It was during this time that I realised the depth of grief and loss I felt with the absence of Auntie Glenda in my life. Long ago, I had realised that lots had to change and be challenged in our auntie-niece relationship, but it did not cancel out the fact that I loved her. Everyone tried to tell me why I should not feel guilty and went through the reasons why I shouldn't feel such a connection with her, but to no avail. I could not just sever that attachment of affection and love, albeit it had begun to feel one-sided.

She had loved me. I knew that. All those years of visiting us and our endless shopping sprees and cream cakes. The Sundays in church together and the variety of trips we went on, just like every other closely knitted auntie and niece. People did not see all that once I'd started to open up about the things Uncle Ivan had done to me. The deeper we delved into the complex workings of our relationship and Uncle Ivan's involvement, the more people seemed to have only disdain for Auntie.

Geoff knew my love for her, and my kids had grown up with her in their lives, but even they did not seem to see the wrenching that the tearing her out of my life had done to me. They had gone into defence mode...defence of me. My children felt a sense of anger towards Auntie as they believed she should have done more to protect me and felt that she should have acted differently once she knew about it all. I, on the other hand, could see that she had let me down, but I could not and would not allow myself to entertain the thought of it all being her fault.

I grieved so much for her. My mum and dad were dead, and every other auntie and uncle had now gone. Auntie

Glenda was my only remaining relative from that generation, and now it felt like my precious auntie was dying. My heart hurt beyond belief as I truly believed I had caused the terrible betrayal she must be feeling. My grief was not for myself...it was for her. I couldn't bear the thought of what her already-bruised heart was going through.

The sadness for Auntie Glenda was something I carried for many more months, and it was heartbreaking that I could not reach out to her. I wanted to with all my heart! I'd sit on her WhatsApp chat writing messages and then deleting them over and over again, just pretending for a moment that I could send them so she could read the truth of how I felt.

I could not rectify this, and that was the hardest thing. I had lived a life of forgiveness and had always done my best to be a peacemaker, but this time I couldn't. The police would look dimly on any contact and, truth be known, I was doubtful she would accept what I wanted to say anyway. I had reported her husband, and I'd heard from others that her rhetoric was that I had made up a whole lot of lies, so it would be futile.

There was nothing easy at all about this whole process. The impact on all relationships cannot be underestimated as family adjust and try to make sense of this insidious thing: sexual abuse.

The repetition of thoughts and thinking processes go round and round in circles where trauma is present. The brain is desperately trying to find a place to settle what's happening by processing it and then tries desperately to store it correctly, only to find it cannot. I felt trapped in a vicious cycle.

My heart had gone through so much, but it was always held in the Father's hands. My relationship with Him could never be severed but, during this time, I couldn't dare accept His love and I locked the doors tight when I felt threatened, scared and misunderstood. It was never long before I cried to Him but then realised that I was so closed off, He could not get through to me.

He could do anything, but the one thing He needed was a part of my heart that was too much to ask. I realised I could not open anything; in fact, I couldn't see any chink of opportunity for the Holy Spirit to seep into my heart. It was firmly shut.

This was the point that I searched my heart and realised I so needed Him but dare not allow it. I could not keep letting Him down. I hated failure and that was something I felt I was living in. I asked the Holy Spirit to search my heart and find the slightest chink of an opening and if He could then, "Please, please, in Your mercy, squeeze through!"

I immediately saw a 'Rizla' paper. These were papers in which my father-in-law used to roll up his tobacco for a cheaper smoking session. If anyone knows about Rizla paper, it's so unbelievably thin - almost see-through. Jesus immediately showed me an opening He could see where you could only get a Rizla paper through. That was good enough for Him and I said, "Ok Lord, please get through it and open up my heart again." That was all He wanted to hear. It took several months for that opening in my heart to get bigger, but it had begun.

## Chapter Thirteen
## River Tay

The weeks were dragging and all I wanted to do was stay in bed. I almost envied those who had that choice. I did not!

Julie would regularly tell me about many of her clients who stayed under the duvet, ate next to nothing and cocooned themselves in hiding, away from the world; after all, most of them had been so hurt by it. The bizarre thing is that bed had not always been a safe place for them, which had been my experience too.

Some of the assaults from Uncle Ivan and Jerry had been in bed, which had invariably built a sense of bed being a necessity rather than a pleasure. Mornings waking in bed are lovely as we are relaxed, warm and, in theory, refreshed. However, throughout my life, I often felt a dreaded feeling at night when all the lights were off and there was movement in the house, or my door was slowly opened...usually by a little one wanting milk or a cuddle, or just Geoff who'd got up for a drink and a Rennie. In years gone by, it was my precious dad just checking in on me as he was on his way to bed.

Unfortunately, at times like this, the traumatised, heightened brain instantly goes into panic mode, and it affects the body instinctively. Everything goes tense, eyes widen and the heart pumps blood faster. On these occasions, I would hold my breath until I was able to rationalise and realise that everything was actually okay.

This damage can stay for years and years and, thankfully, I have learnt that I AM in a safe place and my memories are only feelings and not the reality of today. This is something that Jesus wants us to build our lives on: truth not feelings. I am a chief mistake-maker in this one. My feelings have often been so unbelievably strong and real, but feelings don't set us free; only truth can do that.

DC Gallucci rang me and explained that I had to go to Scotland to see him and listen to my ABE (Achieving Best Evidence) interview in preparation for the trial. I had never met DC Gallucci, and I was nervous. What if I lost my confidence and made a fool of myself? What on earth was he going to ask me?

Ann and I took the long drive to Scotland, talking all the way. There was no way I could eat anything; I had not eaten much at all for the last few weeks. Everyone laughed at my diet, which consisted of anything with anything. I would open the fridge, pick two or three things from whatever was in there and throw them together. Things that I thought would keep me thin, of course. A dish of cabbage, a blob of cream cheese and jalapeños or a handful of peanuts and a fried egg. All perfectly good choices to me but no one else agreed.

Around the time of originally opening up to Rob and Ann, I stopped eating healthily and argued with everyone that it was okay to eat Dream Topping twice a day and nothing else, hence three stone (19kg) dropped off me and my skin looked grey. Those who had no idea about my weird eating just thought I had an excellent diet plan, seeing the results before their eyes. Others that knew me thought it was a rather foolish way to lose weight.

The truth was that I was on an 'angry at me' phase which made me want to starve myself. I was (and still am) an emotional eater and often, when no one is looking, I want to cry as I am putting food in my mouth as I feel out of control. The digestive system is directly linked to our emotions, and we use it to suppress or soothe our emotions.

SCOTLAND! Oh no! That sign. It made me sick as a dog all those years ago, and now even more so as I knew I was willingly returning to lay everything bare before the police and the courts....and Auntie Glenda! I had never been to a police station before, other than for a teenage misdemeanour that Lewis had naively got himself into.

As Ann and I approached the town with the police station, I noticed that we were literally just down the road from the house where all the abuse had happened when I was fourteen years old. We had discussed the possibility of going to see it. I wanted to stand there and think and pray.

We looked at each other and agreed that this was right to do. As we pulled up on the roadside, my heart was racing. It looked just the same - overgrown with bushes but fundamentally the same. We walked cautiously towards the house, and I stopped a distance away, looking at each window, each one representing some abuse and sexual act. It felt surreal and I could hardly believe what was in front of me, yet it was so right to be there. This was my first and last opportunity ever to stand as an adult where I stood as a broken child.

It was as if time stood still, and I could hardly believe I was looking at the house that I had spent years and years trying to forget. I remembered my beautiful mum so happy and enjoying her Scottish holiday; my cousins running round; Auntie watering her sumptuous hanging baskets in the evenings. All those years ago, I could never have imagined it was just down the road from the police station where I would one day talk unreservedly about what was happening to me.

I stood as an adult, but I also acknowledged the fourteen-year-old me who was alone, standing there defenceless and lost. I felt the absolute dread and I remembered the details of his face, his touch, and that traumatised, bereft feeling that each encounter left on me. The times my memories, in recent months, flashed and placed me standing against the wall in his bedroom distressed, utterly shattered and fearful.

Yet today, in this moment, I was not alone, I wasn't defenceless and, above it all, I could feel the healing love of God. I knew all those years ago the Father was right by my side whilst Uncle Ivan made the choices to abuse me. This day, I asked the Holy Spirit to heal me and, as I wept inwardly and silently, I knew that this was a pivotal moment in time where God had orchestrated this painful encounter. It needed to be acknowledged and felt but, more than anything, I so desperately needed to ask the Holy Spirit to bring healing into my heart as I stood where so much death had been sown.

I recalled, all those years ago, a little old lady in church who knew nothing, whispering in my ear, "Somebody has kissed you with death, but Jesus wants to kiss you back to life." I walked away, knowing His Spirit, in that moment, had kissed me. He was on my case and would not stop until I was whole.

We drove out of the village and, to my surprise, past the River Tay, its banks holding so many mixed emotions. My cousin Jenny and I would wander down to the river, sitting on the stone bridge over it, pretending to talk in a Scottish twang and laughing as people passed by. Yet this was also the river I had dived into, anguished and confused, swimming deeper and deeper until I was in difficulty.

I now sat there, remembering and pondering on how blessed I was that I had survived not only the river but also the holiday with Uncle Ivan. I gave that time into the Lord's hands and, surrendering its grief and distress, we drove away to go and face whatever was in store at the police station.

"Are you Pippa?" asked DC Gallucci. He opened the door with a smile, and we walked through for me to sit with him and listen to my ABE interview. This was the first time I had heard it played back to me. DC Gallucci warned me that it can be quite upsetting hearing yourself describing what happened, and he gently pushed the tissue box towards me. Astonishingly, the original uninterrupted recording was two and a half hours long. The CPS cuts them down for court to eradicate all irrelevant information, but it was still an hour and twenty minutes long.

DC Gallucci sat right next to me. I felt uneasy and embarrassed to start off with; these were intimate things but, more than that, they were very detailed and graphic. All my life, I had minimised and tried to make light of everything, but here I was, sitting with a man - a detective that I'd never seen before - who was listening to words no one had ever even uttered in my house as a child! And if I'm honest, as an adult I still cannot say those words! After twenty minutes, I realised he had heard things like this a hundred times over and did not seem to flinch. This was the crux of everything.

I was shocked at what I had disclosed and had forgotten some of the things I'd said. All I could think was, "That poor little girl!" as if it wasn't me. I saw it how others would see it. Then, oh no! I had said things about Uncle Ivan and his manipulative ways. I mentioned the way he had coerced and overridden me. "He will be so angry, so very angry with me!"

I wanted to tell DC Gallucci how scared I was and how intimidated my uncle made me feel, even though he was not there. However, he had previously pre-warned me that I must not speak during this time as everything was being video recorded. That was hard...very hard. I was being recorded whilst watching a recording that contained the worst things that a man did to me.

It was finally over, and I had slouched down in my seat. DC Gallucci was still and upright, patiently waiting for me to stop wiping my snotty nose and pull my dishevelled self together.

As I left the police station for a short break and a cuppa, there was Ann, bags of doughnuts and cookies in one hand and chocolate bars in the other. It didn't take long to work through them all; my nerves were totally on edge and the day was not finished.

Going back into the police station after the break was a challenge. I felt spent on it all and could not help but think about the brave other victims who had got this far and then pulled out due to the emotional, over-demanding process.

Twenty minutes later, I was sitting with DC Gallucci in a video meeting with the CPS Barrister who had made the charging decisions, another couple of people from the legal team and, to my surprise, the amazing Julie! They were all so kind and so supportive.

"Pippa, you will be okay; you really will," they reiterated, all being extremely kind and doing their best to assure me that I would do well in court, and they would be there, backing me all the way.

I pushed to the back of my mind the identical whispers that Uncle Ivan repeatedly uttered when no one was listening: "It will all be okay, Pippa. You will be fine."

## Chapter Fourteen
## On Hold

After six long months of waiting, the trial was upon us, with six days set in the court calendar for the event. Through gritted determination, and an incomprehensible amount of anxiety, this whole journey of the reporting, the arrest, investigation, waiting for the CPS information-gathering and charging decision, then the plea hearing, finally the trial was here! It had been a gruelling wait, especially as this and the second case, involving Jerry, had been running alongside each other.

We had all arrived in Scotland: Geoff and Team Pippa (Rob and Ann, Dan and Sophia) all set to go but not really sure of what laid ahead. Everyone was trying to be positive and pleased...at least we had actually made it!

Geoff had scraped through, living with all the extra pressure that this had brought him whilst losing his brother to cancer. Team Pippa had survived so many wobbles, dramatic meltdowns and endless chats that had gone into the night. I had actually made it too.

We all like to make a good impression by dressing well. Unfortunately, in the distraction and chaos of everything and unbeknownst to Sophia, she had put every item of clothing on back-to-front. The jumpsuit had the baggy bum at the front and her t-shirt was inside out, allowing the label to flap in the Scottish wind. She hadn't noticed at all! Dan was oblivious, too, and they went on their way. It was only when she went to some public toilets to wash her hands and saw her reflection in the mirror, that she realised when she saw *Primark* on the label.

Anyone else would have turned their clothes around there and then but, overcome by embarrassment, she came running out. Much to Dan's mortification, she stripped off in the car in a bustling Scottish car park and redressed herself! And she's a pastor!

Despite the seriousness of the occasion, my Mum had left a legacy of laughter in me, and I couldn't help but see the funny side which lightened the mood momentarily!

I, on the other hand, had arrived with my best clothes which, might I add, were a nightmare to choose. I wanted to be smart, which would give me confidence, and immaculate, which would mean I meant business, but I also wanted to look classy without any hint of 'tarty,' and understated rather than overstated, which meant I did not want to appear overconfident or presumptuous. What do you choose to wear for such an occasion?

I felt the pressure of a jury who would scrutinise what I looked like, how I moved, what I said and how I held or did not hold it together. For me, a lot hung on this. Julie had, on several occasions, emphasised not to go into court with a cocky, angry or argumentative attitude, and not to be 'dolled up to the nines' as first impressions count, "Although they shouldn't!" she always added afterwards. I always wore make-up, regardless of the occasion, so I decided that on that day, I'd be exactly the same; after all, it was my everyday mask, and it gave me confidence.

Everyone had a different idea of what I should be wearing, as usual. It was summer, so I settled for a smart blouse, black trousers and my shiny shoes. My grey roots were dyed and my eyelashes at their optimum after a twelve-week serum application experiment, and I was ready!

I gazed into the full-length mirror as I prepared to leave my hotel room to go. I felt confused by the image looking back at me: someone I recognised but felt I didn't know. My own image, in those few moments, made me feel sad and lost. Everything on the outside was groomed and ready, but everything inside felt groomed for other reasons. I felt a product of other people's choices and I even questioned my opinions of myself. *What was I doing standing here? Why was I in this position?*

I took the deepest of breaths and said out loud, "Come on, Pippa. Jesus is your saving defence and He's with you! Let the court do its job," and off I went.

Geoff stayed at the hotel as he was the second witness and wasn't allowed anywhere near me in court until he had testified. He was due in the witness box the next day. He had borne so much over the years and my heart ached for him as he was incredibly nervous. He would be speaking in front of important people who would be hanging on his every word, and he felt the pressure of 'getting it right.'

We kissed and gave each other a long, knowing hug.

I had 'special measures' so I was to arrive at the court through the side entrance where the Security and Witness Care Team would look after me. We held back in the car before parking. I wanted to see if I could spot Uncle Ivan and Auntie Glenda arriving; I needed to see them, to see how strong they looked. I was desperate for them not to look fragile and old. It was not to salve my conscience, but it was because I genuinely cared and was desperate to know that this journey of justice hadn't been responsible for their demise.

To my astonishment, a car pulled up and Auntie Glenda got out first. She helped Uncle out and, as I watched them climb the steps, I let out a guttural heart-wrenching cry, "Auntie, Auntie! I'm so sorry!" I couldn't hold back my anguish, and I writhed in my seat and in that moment, I felt very, very guilty. I wanted her to hear me; I so wished she could see how very sad I was for her.

Once I had managed to calm down, I was actually surprised to see they had arrived all dressed up in colours that I didn't expect. Auntie was wearing a bright pink jacket and floral, boldly coloured pink and blue scarf whilst Uncle was sporting a petrol-blue jumper over his blue checked shirt. They looked like they were off on a shopping spree.

It helped me. It gave the impression that they were okay, I am sure that was not the case but, for me in that moment, it was what I needed. I pulled myself together and we pulled into the car park for people who had special measures. The seriousness of where we were hit me again as the security guards thoroughly checked every one of us through the scanner and handheld beeper. We emptied our bags and pockets, and we all laughed as, between us, we'd got scissors, an Epipen, lighter and other miscellaneous things that had to be retained. Other than that, everyone was sombre, and I was a bag of nerves.

Eventually, DC Gallucci came and collected me to sit with him and have a final refresher on my ABE interview. He was walking in front of me with a stack of files under his arm and I nervously followed him past all sorts of legal people to the room where we were to talk, watch my ABE interview, and wait for the moment I would be called into court.

Unbeknown to him, he had walked me straight past the room where Uncle Ivan and Auntie Glenda were sitting.

They were near the doorway and, as our eyes locked, it was as if everything suddenly went into slow motion. Auntie quickly stood to her feet, with a wild, concerned look on her face, and looked as if she were about to speak to me. I glanced over at Uncle Ivan, who looked surprisingly well and fresh-faced. It was all too much to take in, and all within a split second. The sight of his big belly reassured me that he was in good health and was not wasting away with worry or old age, but it also triggered a terrifying flashback to seeing that belly all those years ago in the flesh.

I should not have seen them. In fact, I should have been nowhere near them. DC Gallucci was oblivious to this, as he was leading the way and hadn't looked to his left where they were sitting. I rapidly turned away to avoid anything Auntie might say and collapsed in a chair once in our room with the door closed behind us. As I tearfully watched my interview, DC Gallucci must have wondered what on earth was wrong with me until I blurted out that I'd just seen Uncle Ivan. He looked shocked, and apologised, stressing that it should not have happened. It was not a great start, but I had made it there and, any time now, I would be called in!

The clock was ticking and every now and again DC Gallucci got up and went to the door. I couldn't hear the chats he was having, but I started to grow anxious and was too nervous to ask if something was wrong.

I began to notice DC Gallucci having more serious chats with barristers and court officers at the door until, suddenly, the door flung open and my barrister, looking rather burdened, was approaching me with his old, mangled wig and a pile of files tucked under his arm. He didn't have a look on his face that I wanted to see.

"What's wrong?" I blurted out.

"I'm very sorry, Pippa, but today is not going ahead. It's been adjourned." He took his wig off and sat down cautiously, pulling his chair closer to me. DC Gallucci was leaning against the wall with his head down, occasionally glancing at me.

"WHY? Why on earth not?" I cried out in disbelief.

"The defence have claimed that they haven't had all the information until recently, and the other case, Jerry's, has been brought up as a cause for concern."

My mind couldn't take it all in. *What does that mean? What does that have to do with Uncle Ivan?* I was bemused. My barrister went on to explain that the defence needed more time to look at the evidence as it could be said that there were similarities between both cases.

"What? No!" I said, upset and shaken by the news. "Well, yes," I said, "both were sexual but not linked at all. There is no mixing up the men, places and incidents in my mind!" I said with certainty.

My barrister knew that, and he was as upset as I was, but said, "Unfortunately, this is not an uncommon event in the court arena. Cases are adjourned for so many reasons." I was utterly flabbergasted by his next comment: "Pippa, it is being questioned whether the cases could make up a double trial."

I sat, dumbfounded. *How on earth does that work? How could I withstand that?* My nerves would not stand two trials at one time; double the length of time and double everything! I made it very clear that as hard and exhausting as it would be, I needed the trials to be separate. How on earth could I be expected to be cross-examined at the same time on two completely separate lengthy sprees of assaults.

My barrister understood that and said he would do his best to express that to everyone concerned. "Let's let both sides have a few weeks to gather their information and ask their questions and we'll have a legal court hearing to work out our way forward."

It all seemed bizarre, and I felt completely out of my depth. "But he's eighty-five! He will die and it will be too late! He'll never have to give an account for his actions!" I was so concerned by this. In fact, this was all I could think about. I had waited for so long and he was now at the end of his life. *Please, no! Please don't let him die before a trial!*

The barrister took his glasses off and with an incredibly sympathetic voice said, "Pippa, he may die, but let's hope and pray he doesn't." That was no reassurance to me!

Even-so My mum had taught me the height of manners and I knew how to be gracious and amicable, I wanted to act with dignity as I knew none of it was my barristers doing and all he wanted was for it to go ahead. He knew more than anyone that the law has to answer certain questions and be satisfied before a trial can commence and he certainly did not want anything to come up during the trial that could adjourn it again and cause further delay and devastation as we'd waited so long for this. I shook his hand and thanked him sincerely as I knew he would do all he could to fight for me.

I was walked across the building to be with Team Pippa. I couldn't see anything in my peripheral vision or hear anything. My legs were weak, and my strength drained from me. I was in shock, and after all the months and months of waiting, I had just had the carpet ripped away, only to take me back to that same place...waiting again! And for who knew how long! I never even got to go into the court room. At least Uncle Ivan and Auntie Glenda got in there. They were clearly relieved and happy as their side had uttered a hushed but emphatic, "YES!" in relief as the decision was made that it was being adjourned. They had been given more time.

But he's eighty-five! *He will die; it will be too late!* That's how I left the courthouse that day, and the truth of the matter was that no one could guarantee it wouldn't be the case.

Six more tedious weeks passed, and a court hearing was finally held. The date for a six-day trial was set to start in seven months and the idea of a double trial dissipated, to my utter relief.

## Chapter Fifteen
## Take Him Down!

Four days after we had the news that Uncle Ivan and Jerry's trials were to take place separately, Jerry was to enter his plea at a hearing in court. He had said that he was not guilty all the way through the investigation, so surely it would be no surprise as to what he would plea.

The unfortunate and almost incomprehensible reality was that, inevitably, this would mean that a Crown Court trial would have to happen. I would have to stand up in court and be cross-examined on every sordid detail the defence barrister thought fit, to try to catch me out and prove his client's innocence. I would have twelve people scrutinising every word, movement and emotion. I didn't feel strong enough to go through two trials, as I was presuming that Uncle Ivan would also plead 'not guilty'.

To my utter surprise, after a few weeks, DC Hannah called with some unexpected news. Jerry had changed his mind and not only was he pleading guilty, but his sentencing would be brought forward as it would not need to go to trial. He had pleaded guilty to five out of the seven offences. Bizarrely, he'd admitted to being guilty of the most serious charge; therefore, it did not take long for me to agree with the police that this was a good result as he would most probably get a custodial sentence. More importantly to me, though, was that he actually admitted his guilt and it would clear the way for me to focus on Uncle Ivan's prosecution. I certainly didn't feel that I had the strength to fight both!

I did not have long to dwell on it as only three months later, Jerry's sentencing date was upon us!

From the moment I awoke, even before I opened my eyes in the morning, a feeling of dread hit my stomach! The date of Jerry's sentencing was here, and I had got no other experience to compare it with. My only taste of court was the time that I went to watch Jerry at the Magistrates' Court for his preliminary hearing. I knew what respect was, and the importance of following court etiquette, but what really was that etiquette? Be smart, stand for the judge to enter the room and listen very carefully?

I sat there on my own, rubbing my hands together in such a fashion that my wrists hurt. There he was, on a screen. He was appearing remotely, and I braced myself as I looked over towards it. I hadn't seen him since all the incidents had occurred, and he was barely recognisable from the youthful Jerry that I remembered. Seeing him again caused my stomach to churn. As I looked at his face, all I could visualise was his penis: the weapon that had wounded my emotions so deeply. I struggled to see the man...only what he did. His manner appeared cold and callous, and he was only interested in telling the court how ill he was.

The judge was most annoyed that Jerry had attended the hearing remotely and made it clear that regardless of his medical conditions, from that point onwards, he **must** be at the court in person. The hearing was short, to the point, and a tiny taster of how tense thirty minutes in court could be.

Coming home from that encounter, I recoiled into myself, knowing full well that it was just the beginning; up ahead were so many more court hurdles and traumatic challenges. I felt alone on my journey and, although I had Team Pippa (minus Ann, who had to work), Geoff, and a few others, I felt isolated within myself. They could all imagine how I felt, but they could not know exactly. I found myself unable, at times, to express what was going on internally. Things felt out of my control, and I felt incredibly vulnerable. Vulnerable to other people's comments and concerns when they, in fact, hadn't got a clue how to handle trauma or even a court case, never mind two!

Geoff and Team Pippa understood but it felt the circles of understanding were closing in fast, with fewer and fewer people who I felt were safe to talk to.

Everything within me wanted to withdraw, and church was no exception, but I had learnt a long time ago that the one place to be when you are struggling and feeling isolated is to be in church with God's people. This is the place where, even if I felt closed off to others, I was putting myself in a position where I could hear from God and He could soothe me.

The beautiful Bible verse that held me all through the abuse, right through the years and still now as I struggle to be around people, is Zephaniah 3:17 "...*and he will quiet you with His love.*" If I allow his hand to gently rest on me, His gentle, sweet, calming peace invades every dark and troubled thing.

There were choices I could make, and I didn't need to tell anyone anything if I did not want to. This was a vital lesson I so needed to understand. When it all boils down, we all have choices, and we should all have control of our own life. However, when a person has suffered sexual abuse and other forms of trauma, they can get completely lost in the choices that are available to them. A need to please others - and a fear of not doing so – drove me into doing and saying things I didn't really want to do, or even agree with.

In church, this was no exception. I found it so easy to fall into the trap of struggling terribly, broken and isolated inside, and saying nothing...but then I would overshare to some other person who then had no idea what to say and, as a result, said the wrong things. It was like I was tormented, being pushed to and fro, and all the time I just simply needed to feel safe.

..........

The morning of Jerry's sentencing had arrived. This was it...a monumental day! I could hardly believe that the time was here when I would actually see Jerry standing in court in person, in a box under guard, and receiving a prison sentence for his crimes - the things he did to me that I had spent years burying and writing off as 'not that serious'.

These are the five offences to which he pleaded guilty and were accepted for sentencing:

### *Five charges of gross indecency (Indecency with Children Act 1960)*

*- Making the victim show her naked body in bath inciting the victim to wash her breasts and in between legs in bath*
*- Making the victim stand naked whilst brushing teeth and watching*
*- Masturbating on stairs on not less than three occasions (multiple occasions)*

### *Two charges of indecent assault (Sexual Offences Act 1956):*

- *Kissing*
- *Digital penetration of vagina*

The other charges that were agreed to be dropped during the plea bargain were:

### *Two charges of gross indecency (Indecency with Children Act 1960)*

- *Masturbating on stairs (first occasion)*
- *Masturbating on bed*

Team Pippa were with me, armed with tissues and chocolate bars. Breakfast was the last thing on my mind! In fact, I had hardly eaten for a week or more.

We pulled up in the Crown Court car park and I froze. "I can't go in! I can't do it! Don't make me, please!"

Team Pippa in turn each one calmly said, "It's ok. Yes, you can do it. We are together and we are here for you; you're not on your own."

Eventually venturing out of the car, I walked slowly towards the court doors. It seemed a strange world as if everything had stood still and I was the only person moving. My feet felt heavy, and I was breathing shallower and more rapidly than normal. We were quickly escorted into a room to avoid the defendant. It seemed strange calling him that. Suddenly everything and everyone was very serious.

We went into several rooms but finally landed in a little one, where we paced around waiting, and it was as if time stood still. I had been given my Victim Impact Statement

(VIS) by the CPS. The barrister came for a chat with overflowing files under his arm and a robe that could house at least two people. He was kind but I felt the immensity of what was about to happen, and I couldn't fully concentrate on what he was saying.

I read through my VIS again, and it hit me between the eyes. This was what he had done and, undeniably, what he had made me feel like. For the first time, it dawned on me that **this** was no longer lurking in the shadows of Uncle Ivan's crimes **This** had a status of its own. Here we were, purely because of what Jerry had done, and this was my chance to speak out about how he had intimidated and traumatised me repeatedly.

I clutched hold of my mum's handkerchief, hoping so much that she would have been proud of me. Today, I felt like her: incredibly smart and well-groomed, with shiny black patent shoes. Even though people say your loved ones look down on you, I always take the opposite view. I hope that absolutely is NOT the case as I would rather her not see all the struggles that went on down here. Who would want that!

Rob and Dan had very nice jumpers on, and Sophia was dressed in her finest little dress; well, it was bound to be little as she is tiny. We all laughed, commenting of how well we all brush up. Thank goodness Rob hadn't arrived in his jeans that could walk themselves to bed; it was a standard joke...as clean as Rob was, his jeans were only washed when absolutely necessary!

Here we were in the seriousness of a sobering situation, but we had moments of fun and I felt truly blessed that I had Team Pippa alongside me.

We all jumped as Jerry's name was announced over a Tannoy! I panicked, my mouth went dry, and this was it! The CPS woman was standing with her files and the barristers were there with their tatty wigs (a sign that they are experienced). Team Pippa made their way upstairs into the public gallery and I took a deep breath, held it for a bit, and was led into the courtroom. I walked across the room and sat down on my own in the middle of a row of six seats in three rows. This was surreal. I looked up, and walking across the court was Jerry.

He sauntered across to go into the box as if he was casually strolling down the road. I anxiously squirmed in my seat, looking around the room. Sitting completely on my own, I felt incredibly vulnerable. This was a big oversight on the part of the police and the Witness Care Team, as I had been promised that I wouldn't be on my own and that I would definitely have a police officer with me. Unfortunately, this was not the case.

We all stood as the judge walked in the room and then, from that moment, the court was in session. I sat aghast and taken aback by the atmosphere and the seriousness of the proceedings. Of course this was serious, but one could almost literally cut the atmosphere.

I had no idea of the depth of detail into which the judge would go. From the onset, it was very clear that Judge Hall called all the shots and that nothing happened in her courtroom without her permission. She systematically worked through each offence, describing where, when and what had happened. In a meticulous fashion, she unpicked the mitigating and aggravated factors. I felt embarrassed and slightly horrified that it was all said in front of Team Pippa. I guess my reaction was ridiculous, really, as they already knew exactly what had happened; I'd spilled the beans over many chats over the months. There was no place for modesty or shyness in that room.

No one in the court room that day wanted to argue or mess with Judge Hall. She was fearsome and vehemently defensive of my position as an eleven-year-old girl. She made absolutely sure that everyone in the courtroom knew the gravity of what Jerry had done, and she made it absolutely clear she would give the maximum sentence possible in her power.

She left no stone unturned. Did he plan this incident? Was it spontaneous? She made it utterly clear that I had been a vulnerable child away from home, entrusted in his care, young and frightened, and had no defence against a man double my age. I had never felt this sense of public defence before, and it floored me. Tears rolled down my face as I watched the scene unfold in front of me.

Suddenly, it was my turn. The judge changed her tone of voice and softened her speech as she said, "Pippa, are you able to come forward now and read your statement?"

I straightened my lapel and trousers. In one hand, I tightly clasped my victim statement and in the other, squeezed my mum's handkerchief. This was it. After all these years, this was my chance to say the truth of what I felt, having to endure his dirty sessions.

I did it! I shook, I stammered and got emotional, but I did it! It felt so good to lay it all bare...and all in front of Jerry! I didn't look at him, and I don't think I could have done so if I had wanted to.

Leaving the witness box, I made my way to my seat. The judge thanked me and proceeded to pull everything together, explaining that she would give him the maximum sentence by today's standards if she could, but her hands were tied by the law at the time of the offences, which was back in the 1980's. Laws are more detailed now and carry stricter penalties.

Jerry was given three years in prison and a year on licence. He has automatically been put on the sex offenders register and, as several police officers reiterated to me before sentencing, his life will not be the same again as he will be known as a paedophile and a predator.

A surprising thing happened next; Jerry's partner, who had not been in court, and was nowhere to be found when she had her opportunity to say something during the court proceedings, was eventually tracked down and finally came to the stand in clothes that would be more fitting for taking one's dog for a walk as opposed to standing in a Crown Court addressing a judge. She gave a character reference for him saying that she had been ill, and he had looked after her really well. It was both ludicrous and in such bad taste as she showed no decorum or respect for the judge and, as she leant sloppily on the witness box, Judge Hall spoke to her: "Are you fully aware of the gravity of your partner's crimes?"

She replied, "Yes, your Honour, I am!"

The judge then asked what her plans were for the future. She appeared to be unbothered by the question and calmly answered, "I love him, and he's been good to me; he looked after me while I was ill. I'll wait for him."

"Please leave my witness box!" the judge said, in an intolerant manner. It was a bizarre five minutes in court and the only person in the room that didn't seem to grasp the gravity of the situation was her.

The moment came that I had been building up to, and I had no idea how it would play out: the moment Jerry would be taken away. My neck and ears were on fire and my head felt so hot. I was shaking and apprehensive about the finale.

It was the quickest ten seconds but so unbelievably powerful as Judge Hall pointed at him with her arm outstretched and said in a firm, authoritative voice, "TAKE HIM DOWN!" And in a moment, he picked up his small bag and was gone. The Judge said, "It's all over now, Pippa. You can go now." I nodded in a thankful gesture back and stood to my feet.

Suddenly everything went from me, and I collapsed in a heap on the floor, passing out. There had been far too much pent-up emotion, and my brain said enough is enough! I woke to the medics and barristers encircling me. I was dishevelled and incredibly embarrassed...but it was all over.

As the evening set in, so did the guilt. It made me sick in the pit of my stomach; the feeling of pity, and the reality of where Jerry had gone, set in. I became totally consumed by the thought that I could get a cup of tea, make a second one, get back into bed or even just go for a walk if I so desired. He, on the other hand, would be fearful, anxious, lonely and separated from his loved ones. He would be in an awful bed, probably sharing his cell with an obnoxious man, having to follow awful rules whilst looking over his shoulder in case someone had caught wind of his crimes. I could not think about the offences he had committee; all I could see was the man. How wicked was I! So selfish... and there was not a thing I could do to put it right.

The following week was filled with feelings that cascaded over each other chaotically. The more that people tried to help me and give me what they thought was sensible reasoning, the more upset I felt. It was me and me alone that had made the choice to report him. I felt as if my suffering had been nothing in comparison to his and, admittedly, I had gone a bit off-piste in my rationale.

Time is a great thing and, as it passed (a week to be precise), I adjusted. It had not been me that had put him in prison - it was the judge. His crimes had been weighed against the law, and he had lost. The consequences were a result of his actions, which was absolutely obvious to everyone around me, but this involved my heart, not theirs. My heart had to adjust, my emotions had to settle, and my spirit needed to let the Lord speak His truth to me.

Then came another challenge. I knew the papers were interested in running an article about the case, but I was not prepared for the headline!

*"You only cared about your own gratification!"*

Oh, my goodness! I was horrified. Yes, it was what I had bravely said in court as I read out my victim statement, but this felt too public and distasteful to be read in the paper. At least in court it was to a chosen, appropriate group of people.

I had full anonymity, which helped me slightly as no one could identify me, but reading the article made me realise afresh what loss I had suffered at the hands of an abuser. It took seven charges, the case being in court and reading about his guilt and a three-year sentence to make me realise what I had lost.

Jerry will be released in a few years and hopefully, by then, will have grappled with the seriousness, gravity, sin and consequence of his actions. Will he have changed? Who knows! Because of his guilty plea, he will have opportunities to follow programmes, have counselling, and be given tools he can use to help him make the right choices and avoid reoffending.

I finally had to relent my wranglings, admit that this was out of my control, and I handed it all over to Jesus. I handed Jerry over, too, and prayed that he would find a place where he can put this right with God and find forgiveness for himself. This was in the final line that I read out in my statement in court and, oh, how I meant it! Forgiveness is a billion times better than anger and unforgiveness and there isn't one of us that does not need the privilege and liberation that forgiveness brings.

One down and one to go!

Could I really go through all this again and come out the other side?

## Chapter Sixteen
## Two Angels

"Poor, poor Auntie!" Here I was again, going round the same circuit, despite her complete lack of awareness of my suffering and empathy for me. I could still visualise her sitting in my lounge and laughing, eating her daily Kit Kat and thoroughly enjoying my company. I pined for what I had lost, as complex as it was. I loved her and I kept seeing the sister my mum loved and always welcomed to our home with such affection. I could no longer tell anyone my feelings about her; as far as everyone else was concerned, she was complicit and wrongly involved in Uncle Ivan's games.

This thread of loss and sadness continued to weave itself through my thoughts on a daily basis as the court process progressed. Why on earth did I care so much when it was not reciprocated? Love is unconditional and, in my mind, regardless of how she treated me, I cannot stop the strongest emotion in the world...LOVE. How can you just turn it off?

Before I had reported Uncle Ivan to the police, I had written my first book. I hadn't started out writing it as a book, but rather as an account, detailing the string of events and challenges throughout my childhood. This was just for me, and I had absolutely no intention of any other soul reading it. It was written in order to release and unpack the story in the hope that I would find freedom in doing so. I certainly found it a cathartic exercise and it was only as I showed it to

Ann and she read it that she said, "This is a book! You should get it published!" I laughed at her, but she was serious.

I had not gone to school much; I had no qualifications and had no idea of how to create a book, so I was flabbergasted to hear the response of the publisher, who agreed, and said he would love to get my manuscript into print.

I drew the front cover, wanting it to depict my love for Jesus as a little girl and the hours we had spent talking to each other, and then as a teenager who had held it all together whilst hushing any talk or hint of a problem...desperate, yet unable to talk.

Shortly after I had reported Uncle Ivan to the police and the criminal process had begun, I had reached the point where I needed to give consent to the publisher to go ahead and get it into print, but something stopped me. I suddenly wondered if I ought to tell the police that I had written a book, as it had all the details of the crimes in it! I felt nervous - very nervous! What if I jeopardised my chances of the book being allowed to be published? But on the flip side, what if the book would have disastrous consequences for my case? I felt scared and wondered if I had made a huge mistake.

I reluctantly contacted DC Gallucci and explained that I had used pseudonyms throughout the book and no places were the same as I did not want people to be easily identifiable once it was published. I had not wanted to publicly display Uncle Ivan's sordid and dishonourable ways or Aunties nervous complexities, but somehow it felt right to tell my story, letting a voice speak that had been silenced.

He listened and didn't seem unduly ruffled by it but said it certainly could not go into print until the CPS had read it and given their direction. I felt troubled that the police had my book. Now the book was going to be read by the police and the CPS, it made me feel really nervous, uneasy and totally exposed. I was bitterly disappointed that the publication had been put on hold but, as time unfolded, it became clear that it held useful information for the police.

DC Gallucci asked me if all the events concerning the abuse and assaults detailed in the book were an accurate representation of what had happened. I confirmed this to be true and, unbeknownst to me, as part of the investigation, he went on to extract every abusive detail in terms of Uncle Ivan and formed his own copy of my book. I thought my story was a bit of a challenging journey, but his version must have been awful as it had all the soft edges knocked off and only contained the abusive actions, words and sexual assaults from Uncle Ivan.

To my horror, DC Gallucci went on to explain how the defence lawyer would be given my book and there was every likelihood that the defendant, Uncle Ivan, would know about it and potentially be able to read it. This information sent shivers down my spine and caused feelings that I had not expected. I had written this in raw honesty, which included all my thoughts and feelings about what Uncle Ivan did in detail, and how his actions changed me. It was NEVER ever with a view to Uncle being able to access it or have any knowledge about it.

I felt cheated and embarrassed. Why did he have to know? Why, when he had ruined so much, did he have to ruin my chance to tell my story whilst I thought I was protecting it by keeping it anonymous! Now it wasn't protected; it was going to be paraded before **his** eyes and his legals' eyes, who may misunderstand my reasons for writing it! I felt like I had been smacked in the face.

As time progressed, I accepted the need for them to read it and hold it. I had to trust God In all the details; He could see the end from the beginning, and my written journey through all this was peppered with the saving grace of Jesus. Therefore, the detective, the CPS and the defence barristers would all get a true sense of who I was and what had happened to me and, more importantly for me, they would hear about Jesus. The CPS held it and, as the case unfolded, there were many legal wranglings over it, right up until till the conclusion of the case.

I often tried to remember a time before strife and personal anxiety. When did it really start? I want to say I can remember and try to pin it onto one event or time but, as soon as I do, I am reminded of other things that happened before that event.

Uncle Ivan's abuse had certainly sunk deep into my subconscious and caused a nervousness and insecurity that was firmly embedded. Jerry and the bicycle man, who had also abused me, had all fed into that too. However, the fight to breathe and survive all the hospital encounters had also been a part of who I was, from a few months old. Even at the very beginning of my life, there was a battle in the incubator.

There was, therefore, no wonder that all this anxiety and fear had flooded into my body and caused it to react. I have always battled with chronic fatigue and a lack of stamina, but this now felt even harder. As I waited, and the trial was put back, the agonising waiting started all over again, and my body started to object. Slowly, all the physical pains which had intermittently afflicted me for years seemed to all unite in one big revolt. My back, shoulders and neck stiffened to such a point that I could not move my own head, and the pain in my legs and hips was unbearable. What was happening to me?

I ended up at hospital in Accident and Emergency, having thorough investigations and scans, and a cocktail of pain medication which made absolutely no difference. I had no idea that trauma could tip into the body, afflicting any or every part. Delayed responses to extreme trauma can cause intense persistent fatigue, sleep difficulties and disorders, depression, nightmares and flashbacks. These, in turn, can trigger pain in the body as muscles tighten and the stresses of the unmanageable emotion can take its toll.

Years of avoidance of dealing with trauma and the emotions, triggers and associations that it brings can not only lead to the mind being exhausted, but the body too. I was learning that, in addition to my body and mind being significantly affected by the current events, the immediate aftermath and (lack of) handling of my childhood abuse was also having a knock-on effect, bringing me to a new low.

Anyone who suffers any form of sexual abuse or sexual assault is also affected by the direct response of others, following the event. Should the victim receive immediate and appropriate help and support, the long-term chances of recovery are greater. However, in many cases victims are alone. Their assaults are unseen and hidden, just as mine were. With no opportunity to release the anguish and trauma, this is often stored in the body, causing physical and mental injury which can become evident much further down the line.

My saving grace was the sustaining and preserving presence of Jesus. He was my bolt hold that was immovable; yet, at times, that truth became hazy and hard to see during this waiting period.

Subconsciously, I had a desire to be numb, which created a lack of focus and motivation. My brain felt incapable of making decisions and I was worried that I was losing my mind because my memory seemed to revel in remembering nothing and feeling nothing. I seemed to dip in and out of this as the months passed by. The details and memories felt jumbled, and it was easier to not feel anything.

On the flip side, when the periods of numbness subsided, I was overwhelmed with emotion and my mood and resolve was just as unpredictable. Geoff and I were exhausted as we were constantly living in survival mode.

Julie was advocating and giving regular updates to DC Gallucci on how I was. At this time, she became very concerned and told the police that the trial MUST go ahead this time as she was not convinced that I could handle another setback. During one of her regular phone call sessions, she'd caught me rambling and distressed. I felt I could not handle any more uncertainty, and I was on the brink of jacking it all in! These were tough weeks, and Julie is the proof that without an ISVA, many a victim would pull out and be another statistic that could not stand up to her abuser.

During our usual Thursday church group, my friend Mick came and sat down next to me. "Pippa, I want to share something I really feel Jesus wants you to know."

He had tears in his eyes, so he got my attention immediately. He knew about the approaching trial and knew I was incredibly nervous. "When you walk into the courtroom, Jesus wants you to know that He's appointed two angels, and they are already there waiting for you. If you look for them, you will see them." We both cried. It would have been impossible for me not to, as I had felt that Jesus had been part of every single turn and outworking of this case, so why would He not be there along with His angels on that day and for the duration of the trial?

I knew His word that He promises never to leave us or forsake us and, again, I was reminded of the scripture in Psalm 28:8: *"He is a saving defence for his anointed ones."* I truly felt the privilege of being in His family. I had chosen Him and, although the Lord's promises are accessible to everyone who calls on Him, He will resist the proud and those who stand against His children.

I had, all those years ago, made the choice to follow Him. He has never failed me and the knowledge of Him appointing angels to guard me in the courtroom meant they would prevent demons from whispering lies and, as a consequence, prevent the truth from being heard. God had my back.

## Chapter Seventeen
### Copious Burps

He lived! Uncle Ivan had made it to the day! He was eighty-six years old, and my biggest fear had been alleviated. The police and barristers all knew the trial had to go ahead this time as I was in a fragile state, and it was doubtful I would be able to continue should there be another adjournment. Julie had got me to this point through some close shaves and we could not afford another one. I'd had the call on the Friday from the CPS and Julie to say that Monday was ON! The trial was all set.

"Everyone is ready, Pippa, and all you have to do is TELL THE TRUTH!" was the message from my whole team.

I hoped that all the questions, wranglings and arguments that were battered about between the prosecution and defence lawyers the last time we were in court were ironed out and everyone was ready for the fight. For me, the fight was to be heard; for every anguish he put me through to be shown in its honesty...but, for Uncle Ivan, his fight was for his freedom.

The evenings before the trial were spent shared out between Team Pippa; I could not get through one without their encouragement. After all, they had got me to this point. We laughed as Ann expressed that she loved a challenge, and I think **I** was that challenge more often than I would like to admit.

I got up on the morning of the trial at 04:30. There was no chance of a restful lie-in; my head was a shed...one like Geoff's (an over-full cluttered mess). Team Pippa had all stayed in the hotel the night before, in preparation for the big week. Unfortunately for Sophia, I had kept her up until midnight the night before we left, trying to iron out my fears which, in true fashion, went round in circles. Only in the doing would it become clear what would unfold and how I would handle it.

This was it! No turning back and, whether I was ready or not, this was happening. We had managed a giggle, as Sophia and I cannot go long without one, even in the midst of the eve of one of the most harrowing times of my life.

Geoff and Team Pippa were meeting for a hearty breakfast. I couldn't swallow a thing; even my antihistamine stuck to the sides as it went down. I don't think I have ever felt so nervous and unprepared for anything! The next few days were about to change my life, and the result would be catastrophic for one of us. I felt sick and could not sit or stand still.

My resolve and fight had waned a little; I felt weaker and less confident. I had my olive-green blazer on, teamed with black blouse and trousers, and had polished my black patent brogues again, as last time was for Jerry's court sentencing. To finish off, I had Mum's handkerchief in my hand, which had a little embroidered flower on the corner and a delicately written *MUM*. Despite this, I did not feel as well-groomed as I had the first-time round.

I couldn't bear to think about my precious dad. How on earth would he have coped with the knowledge of such devastating events, and how would he view me now? Court would probably be the last place he would go. He would do everything in his power to defuse a situation rather than highlight and expose it. His only time in court was when he stood as a conscientious objector in the war and refused to fight as it was his firm conviction that he could not kill another man, regardless of the reason for the battle. He always said how would he ever know if the enemy was a Christian, like himself, and he could never kill a follower of Jesus Christ. I always felt proud of him for that! Many called him a coward and he was stoned as he walked out of the courthouse, but to stand against the crowd and honour your own conviction seemed like the hilt of bravery to me.

Now, as I thought of my dad, I felt shame and grief deep inside - the same shame I felt during Uncle Ivan's 'sessions' as I thought of my dad, desperate for him to come and rescue me, but horrified at the very thought of him knowing what had happened. However, one thing was a fact: my dad had adored me, and that was enough in this moment. He stood in court for what he believed was right, so here I was doing the same! "Thanks Dad," I said under my breath.

I took one last look at myself in the full-length mirror before I stepped out of the hotel room. Geoff walked me down to meet Team Pippa in Reception. It felt like I was walking towards the lion's den, totally unprepared for what it was really like to be the victim in court. Again, Geoff was not allowed to come to court as he was a key witness and had to wait for his allotted time. Poor Geoff was a bag of nerves for both of us; he had journeyed this with me for thirty-nine long years.

As I entered the restaurant, there was my team, standing eagerly, waiting for me with everyone looking well-turned-out for the occasion. However, looking into everyone's faces, I saw concern and felt incredibly sad...sad to put my closest friends in this position. However, I knew they would defend me to the maximum degree, and they were set to be, and do, everything I needed, even sit through a gruelling Crown Court trial for rape of a minor. They wanted to see justice served as they had seen the immense damage that Uncle Ivan had produced in me.

Months before, I had been told that I was not allowed to sit and watch the trial. This was something I found very, very difficult. The worst moments in my life were about to be explained in great detail, and a jury of twelve, a judge, several barristers, court officials, probably Auntie Glenda, and some of my cousins would all hear the horror of it. To top it all off, Uncle Ivan would be sitting through the whole thing. He had get to hear it all. How could that be fair? I did not get the chance to know how the case was presented, what Uncle Ivan said in his defence, and who his witnesses were, or if he had any at all! On top of that, I would not know what my witnesses were saying! Even Geoff couldn't tell me what he had said in his statement. This was something I could not understand, and I had asked Julie on several occasions if there was any way round it.

I had 'special measures' which meant I was protected, where possible, from any contact or sight of the defendant. He, in return, could not see me. Julie had explained how the jury would look dimly on me being present in court in the clear view and presence of the defendant if I had said I needed special measures. It was somewhat contradictory in the eyes of the court.

My rationale was that although I would find it unbelievably difficult to see his face throughout proceedings, it was during the cross-examination where I needed the special measures, as I would be directly talking about what he had done to me whilst he was looking at me. I saw them as two distinctively different things. However, it was explained to me that the court would probably not see it like that.

Julie could understand, to a point, but explained patiently, several times, that it was vital that we did not jeopardise or compromise the case in any way. I accepted the reasoning reluctantly, so then we hatched a back-up plan.

Team Pippa got me to the court and delivered me to the side entrance to be looked after by the Victim Care Team under the rules for special measures, and they all went into court. Fortunately, I was allowed to have trusted friends sit through as much or as little as I wanted, and they were allowed to feed back to me what had been said as long as nothing was recorded or written down.

Rob's intelligent understanding of what was being said, Ann and Sophia's observations of who said what and how they acted, and Dan's astute memory all worked together to glean what they could, so that they could feed back to me. This felt, to me, like the best alternative. I knew they would take in as much as they possibly could to be able to give me a full picture of how the trial was laid out and how it unfolded.

Once through the special measures entrance and security, Team Pippa were down the hallway to the courtroom for the start of the trial. I sat in a rather hot room with Julie and DC Gallucci, experiencing the fact that the heating system had its own issues. I had been warned it could be after lunch that I would take the stand, so I did my best to be patient and go with the flow.

The flow was not flowing. It was stressful, and my stomach had a will of its own. I had never belched so much in my life. It was both embarrassing and funny. Julie said she'd had other victims who could not stop burping! I'm not sure whether I believed her or not, but my nerves were definitely in my stomach. Maybe the endless pellets of chewing gum didn't help! This is when I discovered that the serious, professional DC Gallucci was human, and very easy and comfortable to talk to and be around. His investigation now complete, here we were, sitting together, waiting for something that was out of both of our hands. His relaxed manner and casual chat helped to ease the tension I felt, although the hideous burping continued, to my embarrassment!

Julie was her usual hilarious self as she recounted endless cases she had worked on (some with DC Gallucci) and the crazy, unbelievable things that had happened. Fights, furious knitting, picnics, catheter bags needing changing and even, bizarrely, defendants who limped fragile into court and needed constant ten-minute breaks, only to be found outside walking briskly and intentionally for fag number twenty! Oh, and the antics of the victim's and defendant's families in court with no awareness of court etiquette or expectation. The moments of laughter between us broke up the hours of tension nicely.

The minutes ticked into hours, and it became clear that I would be coming back the next day. The legalities and decisions on what was admissible and relevant for use in this case was taking some working out. I had no idea of what the hitch was.

Day two came and went with mounting tension and burping, waiting all day in vain for my turn on the stand.

Day three arrived after a series of events including the judge having to conclude another case on the Monday morning, the opening of the case against Uncle Ivan, and sleeping overnight on a decision about whether 'the phone call' was able to be used as evidence or not.

The wait was worth it. The judge agreed that the phone call could be played in court, to which our side were delighted. He also agreed that my book would not be used in court, which delighted me even more when I found out, as it was always my hope that as much of it as possible would be protected and private from "the other side". I had already asked the CPS to redact the title as it would make it harder to find. At the time, this mattered so much to me, but now, after many months, I feel free to let my story be open to all. After all, it's the truth…and it being in the open is setting me free.

This was my moment…!

## Chapter Eighteen
### The Stand

At 11.18 a.m. on the third day, the court official opened the door and slowly peered round. "It's time, Pippa. The court is ready for you."

I suddenly felt incredibly vulnerable and scared. Julie grabbed my hand and did not let go until I was sitting in the witness box. "We can do this...we'll do it together!"

I was led to a room adjacent to the court room where my barrister, a very calm and reassuring man, came in to bolster my confidence, alleviate my nerves and give me one final moment before I went in. He had a lovely face and reminded me of my precious Uncle Ray, with a rather a cheeky smile. I saw it first-hand on day one, when he came in to ask me about Auntie Glenda. In all his years doing the job, he had never been in a position where the defendant's wife had made a beeline for him and introduced herself! "It's a rare thing for the defence side to come and introduce themselves to the prosecution lawyer, especially in a case like this!" he said with one highbrow raised in a gesture of disbelief.

"That's Auntie Glenda!" I replied.

He went on to ask, "How blind is Uncle Ivan?"

"I know he is registered as blind but to what degree, I have no idea," I replied.

I wanted to be fair and certainly have never wanted anything otherwise, but I knew that during a recent auntie's funeral, he was overheard commenting on how well the hall was decorated, yet when he was sitting in everybody's company he acted as though he couldn't see anything. He even dropped a full sandwich on the floor and stood on it, pressing it into the carpet, whilst asking where Auntie Glenda was as she stood nearby.

"Interesting," replied my barrister, and there it was...his wry, cheeky smile!

As I walked into the courtroom, my legs felt weak and, holding Julie with one hand, I ran my other hand along the rails. I was led straight into the witness box, and I had walked right by Team Pippa, but I hadn't seen them at all as everything seemed to be in a haze. They were sitting only a couple of rows behind me.

As I sat there stunned, there seemed so much activity around me. The judge, jury and defendant weren't yet in the court, but the officials and barristers were finalising the positioning of the screens and making absolutely sure I could not see where Uncle Ivan would be sitting. They kept looking across at me and asking if I was ok, nodding and giving me reassuring looks. I kept thinking of what my barrister had said just before I walked in: "When you're stressed, rub the palm of your hand with your thumb. It's what I do, and it helps me!"

As I sat there, waiting for the court to settle and for the entrance of the judge, I spoke to Jesus. "Lord, You told me that two angels have been appointed to be in court. Where are they?" I looked round and couldn't see them. "Lord, you promised I'd see them! Where are they" I questioned, puzzled.

He immediately answered, "Just wait a little longer and I'll show you."

The court were all asked to rise, and the judge walked in the room in his red and black gown with an air of importance. Everyone nodded and respectfully resumed their positions. He sat down and looked straight at me. Smiling, he asked if I was ok.

"Yes, thank you," I replied as I took another deep breath, hardly able to take in the situation.

He then went on to explain to me that I had all the time I needed and if I needed to stop or take a break, he would allow that as many times as it was required. I noticed his body language as he leaned forward; his head tilted and, with direct eye contact, he spoke with gentleness, while also commanding the full attention of the court. I felt that God had hand-picked the perfect judge to oversee my case; he had the highest jurisdiction yet every time he spoke to me, I felt valued and respected.

Once he was happy that I was as settled as possible, he then told the officials to bring in the defendant. My knees were shaking, and I didn't know what to do with my hands as I couldn't keep them still. I heard a kerfuffle as Uncle Ivan was led into the glass box by his security guard and stumbled slightly. As I heard him shuffling across the floor, it gave me a pang of guilt. His voice sounded muffled, but it still sent shivers down my spine, hearing it again.

Once all had gone silent in the room, the judge ordered the court officials, "Bring the jury in."

As they filed into the room in a very orderly manner, I looked at each face. At that moment, the Holy Spirit spoke to me and said, "I didn't appoint two angels, I gave you twelve...here they are!" I felt choked! The High Court judge may have chosen them, but the highest judge of Heaven appointed them in His grace and mercy for me.

I swallowed down overwhelming emotion as I knew they were responsible for the course of my life from this point onwards, and also for the consequences of Uncle Ivan's should he be found guilty. They were my angels, and I felt a surge of confidence as I remembered the scripture, *"He is a saving defence to his anointed ones."*

In preparation, weeks before, Julie had told me to look at each jury member and find a face that I could focus on throughout the duration of my time in court. "It may help," she said.

The very first one was the one! He looked kind, had a smart haircut and a tidy round-necked navy jumper. He was fairly young, yet I felt he looked compassionate and genuine. Not really something you could ever know just by observing, but his kind face was enough for me, and I had made my choice.

I felt peculiar and uneasy, not sure what facial expression I could or should give. I felt I owed them something and I wanted to smile at them or at least acknowledge them with a slight nod or something, but every time I looked at one of them, their eyes immediately diverted away from me. It happened with each one I managed to lock eyes with. Consequently, I felt embarrassed and uneasy as I realised the majority of them probably had no idea what to think and had never been in a court situation like this before. A wave of shame washed over me as I wondered what they saw when they looked at me.

After my barrister had opened up the cross-examination and spoken to me with a few opening remarks, Uncle Ivan's barrister stood to his feet and took over. My confidence drained and I felt my insides start to shake. My shoulders started to jump, too, as though something powerful was surging through my body. Adrenaline, anxiety, and the memories of what he did all blasted together in the knowledge that Uncle Ivan was just a few steps away.

All the attention and everyone's eyes were on me. You could hear a pin drop, and everyone was poised ready. This was the monumental moment that I had desperately prayed would happen, and simultaneously dreaded.

The direction in which his questioning started both confused and surprised me. I had imagined and rehearsed so many different questions and scenarios and tried to imagine all the different tactics that he would use to trip me up, but his line of questioning was different to all of them.

"So, Pippa," he began, and proceeded to start at the very first incident, describing the entire event in detail. I listened intently to try to notice any inaccuracies, but there weren't any!

He recounted the first sexual assault by Uncle Ivan when I was six years old, describing it exactly as I had said it had happened and that, in itself, perplexed me. Then, in one short, precise and confident way, he paused, tilted his head and said, "But that didn't happen did it, Pippa?"

"Yes! It did happen!" I replied, quickly.

He continued to go through several incidents exactly as they had happened and then concluded by repeating the same sentence.

All I could say was, "Yes. Yes, it did happen!" It felt like a weak and unconvincing attempt, on his part, to win over and persuade the jury. In my view, all he had succeeded in doing was reminding them of the facts that had already been laid out by the prosecution barrister. Repeating them did not make sense to me from a defence perspective and then to just end his point by saying, "But it didn't happen, did it?" seemed odd. However, I felt that my answer was pathetic and far from adequate too.

Once he'd exhausted that line of questioning, he went on to try and discredit my memory by saying my mum had been with me on that first holiday. Of course, I disputed that she had been with me as I had been in Uncle Ivan and Auntie Glenda's sole care.

He said, "But that simply isn't true is it Pippa? What mum would not go with her six-year-old on holiday, especially given that it was so far away?"

I struggled to respond. The fact was that she had not gone with me and, as far as I remembered, it was a normal and exciting thing to do to go and stay with your favourite auntie, even though it was two-hundred miles away. It was expected that she would have cared for me just as she should, and my mum would have not questioned that. He laboured the point, and I felt like I was waning in my explanation.

He then talked about the car journey home when Uncle Ivan drove. It had just been the two of us, but the barrister had insisted that my mum had accompanied me on the journey too. When he was getting nowhere with that point due to my resolute denials that she had even been on the holiday, he changed tack. "Can you be certain that you were on your own with him? Surely Auntie Glenda took you home too? Why would she not?"

"No," I objected, "she wasn't there."

The barrister said, "But you were in the back. That's because she was in the front."

"No, she wasn't! Why then did I put my hands between my knees as they were banging together and I held them there all the way home because I was so fearful? If Auntie had been in the car, I would not have been in such a state!"

Under my breath, I could not hold back. I needed the Holy Spirit to help me and, as usual, I had barely finished asking before He came to my aid and instantly brought to mind the first time I was rocking backwards and forwards, distressed in my bed with gut wrenching cries of, "Mummy, Daddy, Jesus," over and over again, well into the night until exhaustion took over.

I lifted my head and looked straight in the barrister's eyes and said, "If my Mum had been with me on that holiday, then why did I do this in desperation? Had she been there, my cries would have not been desperate or even needed. I would not have willed everything in me to be heard by my mum, two-hundred miles away, desperate for her to sense I needed her."

He quickly moved on and changed his line of questioning. He reminded the court that I had chosen to forgive Uncle Ivan for what he had done to me. Then, looking around the room in a slightly belittling and disparaging way, said, "So where's your forgiveness now then?"

This felt like the perfect question for me; I knew the answer and knew from the depths of my being that I was qualified to respond to such a question as my life was built on forgiveness. He asked it as though I had no grounds to claim that I had, indeed, forgiven him, as here I was in court, accusing him.

I said, "Jesus!" under my breath. I wanted to do justice to my answer. Team Pippa told me afterwards that they had heard me whisper His name.

"Yes, I have forgiven him, but you need to understand what forgiveness is." I looked intently into the Barristers eyes. "Forgiveness means that I don't hold any anger or bitterness in my heart towards Uncle Ivan, but what I do still have is a lot of pain and sadness. He needs to be held to account for what he did because what he did was a crime, and I need it to be acknowledged so I can go on to live free from this pain and be able to receive total healing."

The barrister didn't say a word and he moved quickly onto the next point. I felt that answer was in the bag, so to speak. As he began to go into some of the events that I had talked about in my police interview, the shaking and trembling was becoming unbearable. I started to feel incredibly sick, and I couldn't help but keep putting my hand over my mouth to stop myself from retching and vomiting. I spilled the glass of water in front of me and nervously mopped it up with the tissues provided.

The judge stopped the barrister and asked me if I needed a break. The relief I felt was enormous. "Oh yes! Yes please!" I answered, in desperation. He cleared the courtroom promptly and Julie quickly came to my assistance. She had been sitting immediately behind me and had been bracing herself to jump in and help me as soon as she was given permission.

I grabbed her and we stumbled out of court together. The Witness Care Team and court officials were there immediately. As I stepped into the hallway, I burst into tears and fell into Julie's arms.

She held me as I sobbed and kept saying, "I'm doing rubbish! I'm ruining it!" I felt like a little girl, lost and scared.

They took me into an adjourning room and sat me down so I could get my breath and calm down. In a seamless flow of confidence, motivation and support, each one gently gave me the strength I needed pull myself together enough to go back into the courtroom. Julie was for me, in that moment, a mum and a fierce defender. She walked me back to court and got me back in the witness box ready for round two, squeezing my hand all the way and whispering, "You can do this; you've got it!"

However, within moments, my anxiety was through the roof again. I wondered how many more points the barrister wanted to raise. Once the judge had clarified with me that I was in a position to begin, the defence barrister started his next lot of questions.

He launched into the events that found me in the bathroom, aged six, in what I had described as a desperate situation. Uncle's barrister cast aspersions on my description of the events. He questioned the whole regime of creaming my eczema. He wanted to know why Auntie wasn't doing this and how often I needed this to happen. He cast doubt on the events by asking what Uncle would ever be expected to help in this way?

All I could say was that I remembered that was Uncle Ivan had talked about checking my eczema and had, on occasions, asked me to turn round or lie down so he could check it. It ran in a long line on my right leg from my ankle all the way up. I relayed that I could always keep my pants on when my daddy had creamed me.

The defence barrister badgered me, wanting me to relent and say that this didn't happen. But how could I? Uncle always used my eczema as an excuse to 'look' at me.

All I remembered from after the horrific bathroom event was that I was hiding naked, curled up behind the toilet, scared and not knowing what to do next or how to get out of the distressing situation I was in, then cleaning up the sick that was in the bath.

The barrister did his best to discredit what I was saying but all I could say was the truth. I had not been able to remember all of the incident in detail due to the level of trauma involved, but I could clearly remember enough detail and knew for certain that I had ended up in a very desperate situation needing help and protection. By now, my whole body was shaking violently again, and my teeth were banging together. I felt utterly out of my depth and wrung-out, emotionally.

I explained how I had ended up in bed, having emptied my case of all my clothes and had put them all on before going to the bottom of my bed under the covers. I did not remember getting from the bathroom or, indeed, getting dressed as my memory only kicks in at the point where I felt safer and clothed.

I was experiencing trauma by this stage of questioning, and as the barrister tried to pick holes in my explanations, I felt anxiety to the point where I wanted to run. It took all my strength and willpower to stay sitting in the seat. My nose and the front of my face went stone cold, and everything was shaking. I started to retch, and my stomach started lurching.

The judge stopped the court promptly and Julie swiftly came to me to help me. He quickly emptied the court, and I was taken out again. I remember feeling a pang of guilt that Uncle Ivan would have to be disturbed and led out again. The complexity of my ambivalence evident...feeling terrified of him whilst also feeling sorry for him!

I stumbled and could not walk straight as the emotions and the atmosphere were all too much. I will never forget Richard, who was one of the Victim Care Team. He followed me into the room and, as I looked up, he had tears rolling down his cheeks. He was visibly moved by what had been discussed in court and he said how very sorry he was that I had endured that as a child. He said that he was rarely like that, but my case had deeply impacted him.

My barrister came in and I burst into tears, saying, "I'm making the worst mess of this! I can't carry on with it."

He spoke to me as though it was a casual afternoon off with nothing pressing to do. Such was his sensitive and clever way of disarming my tension, he managed to talk me round. With Richard and Julie, a massive blow of my nose and absolutely no lipstick left on, I stood up and we walked back in for round three.

This time, as I went in, I noticed Team Pippa. I walked straight passed them and managed to look up into their faces. It was another kindness of God that they had not been asked to leave the court when I left, so it meant they were there when I returned, which comforted me deeply to see them. I think the judge allowed that to help boost me to be able to carry on.

Uncles Ivan's barrister revisited the first incident. He said a string of things that simply weren't true. I was flabbergasted at how ludicrous some of Uncle's explanations were. As a little girl of six, I vividly remember the first time he touched me. I remember where he sat, what he was wearing, what I was wearing and the phone conversation he was having with his son whilst using his other hand to do things to me. How could I ever forget the telephone table he was sitting on and what he was saying during the assault. I felt sick; so very sick.

The barrister continued by moving on to describe the assaults I had endured at fourteen years of age and launched into saying that the room in which I had said the rape had happened did no't actually exist! In my eyes, this was an easy one because it simply did. The barrister questioned what was in the room and I responded with an exact description, which was easy for me: a catty-corner TV and a two-seater settee opposite. I had logged it years ago as the details of that room had traumatised me and were imprinted on my mind.

He insisted that these items had not existed, and that the layout of the house was also different to how I had described it. This, in fact, annoyed me, as he had never even stepped foot in the house but there were countless times that I had wanted to escape from it.

As he started to move on with his questions, I said, "Please may I say something?"

"Well yes," he replied.

"I can tell you the full layout of the house."

I proceeded to do so, and he said, "Ok, that's enough."

"But I haven't finished yet," I retorted! For a moment, I forgot that I was in court and that there were rules. I was overriding his questioning on this matter, and I felt indignant. He had brought it up, so I refused to be bullied into not being able to respond with a full answer. I knew the exact layout of that house, and I was determined to have my say. After all, I knew that Uncle Ivan knew, Auntie Glenda knew and two of their adult children, who had come to court, all knew the layout of this house too and they knew I was giving a one hundred percent accurate description.

I went on to give an exact portrayal of the positioning of every room upstairs, refusing to budge on the details because I had encountered too many incidents in those rooms. No barrister could weaken my resolve in this, but I felt I was fighting for my life. I cannot remember how the cross-examination ended and what happened in the immediate moments afterwards, but I had done it!

The full cross-examination lasted for three hours.

Team Pippa and Julie walked me out of the side entrance and, as we were walking round the front of the building, my strength just drained, and I passed out. I was a dishevelled mess on the curb, highly embarrassed and overwhelmed by what had just happened.

Then suddenly, out of nowhere, the smallest and kindest court official rushed out to see what was happening as he had seen the commotion. He got down and checked me over and said, "Oh dear, she's bumped her head," as he felt several lumps.

"No, no! They're my hair extensions!" I rather groggily answered, chuckling.

## Chapter Nineteen

## Dirty, Grotty Place

I was done! Geoff had completed his questioning and, finally, my other witnesses (my GP and my old friends, Matt and Anna) had also taken their turn in the witness box, giving their accounts of the jigsaw pieces they had.

All that was left was for Uncle Ivan and any of his witnesses to take the stand. It was his opportunity to try to keep the truth of what happened in the dark and try to make everyone believe something that hadn't happened.

I had been strongly advised not to be in court, so I needed a plan as I felt desperate to know what his defence was. I needed eyes and ears to be there in court. That came in the form of Team Pippa. They were all in agreement to go, but we realised that I would be on my own back at the hotel. Geoff was already on his way home as he had done his bit, which had apparently gone well. Fortunately, he had got away with getting mixed up with how long we'd been married and had made a joke about it in the box (which is not allowed, but in his cheeky way he had got away with it).

He was utterly relieved when it was over as he had lived thirty-six years of it and had just had to relive its effects all over again in court. He just wanted to get back home to de-stress as it had taken a toll on him. Unfortunately, Dan and Sophia had to go home too, at this point, which meant that only Rob and Ann were available to go and listen to Uncle doing his bit in court. However, I had every confidence in them that they would glean all the information I felt I needed.

I was a huge mixed bag of feelings, which ranged from absolute fear of him sabotaging everything I said, to him making up a completely outlandish story that sounded totally believable. Did he have character witnesses? If so, who would they be? He had probably be able to provide some really high and mighty ones at that! He was used to talking to people and giving instruction and guidance, as he had spent his whole life being an authority-figure and, in honesty, he usually had an audience. Would his charisma come to the forefront and his confidence hoodwink and delude everyone?

I wondered if he could even remember all of what he had done to me. One thing I truly believed was that Uncle Ivan didn't have a flicker of a doubt that he would win. I could see him with his shoulders back, chest out and his sardonic laughter which reaffirmed his arrogance. All I had to do was hang in there and wait, and all would be revealed once they returned.

I waved off Rob and Ann in the car park as they went to court. Standing there, I felt a perturbed, foreboding feeling. I had laid it on thick that I had be absolutely fine on my own, but it scared me, and I just wanted to be held. I stood looking at the dirty, mossy-green buildings that surrounded me; they all looked like they'd needed jet-washing for the last fifteen years. Everything looked drab and unkempt. "What a grotty, dirty, miserable-looking place!" I said to myself under my breath, and it fit perfectly with the grotty, dirty, miserable situation that Uncle Ivan had put me in.

Auntie Glenda and two of their adult children and a partner were back in court to support Uncle Ivan. My cousins looked drawn and drained by the seriousness of things. Thet gave a slight nod of acknowledgement when they caught the eye of Ann; certainly not of anger, but just deep sadness.

Auntie had been heightened and obviously upset, especially as the details of the abuse were described in court, and as she had gasped and made comments, she had been reprimanded for her reactions and told to remain silent. Poor Auntie! I could barely dare to think about what they were all going through now, having heard every shred of evidence in sordid detail from several sources and angles. I was their family…someone they had loved. How on earth could they bear to hear all the things their dad/husband did to me and made me do? It was all so shocking.

At that stage, I believed that now we were at the end of the case, they must be utterly broken and devastated by what they had learned about their father and husband over that week. I hoped that at some stage in the future, this would lead them to be able to tell me how deeply sorry they were for what he had done. I did not consider the fact that they might completely believe their dad and hate me for what they thought I was putting their elderly father through.

Auntie had certainly known that some things had happened, and their daughter also knew that something had happened, but I was sure it that it was all a complete shock to his son. Poor Stanley, especially as he had heard in court that the very first assault on me was during a phone call between him and his dad.

My barrister began, and it appeared as though the questioning had not started as he cleverly made what seemed like an off-the-cuff remark to Uncle Ivan. "I bet you couldn't believe your luck when Pippa returned to your house when she was fourteen!"

Uncle Ivan was caught off-guard and gave a slightly audible fleeting laugh and gestured agreement, tipping his head back slightly before realising what his response should have been and replying with a slightly awkward, "No, not at all."

Everyone in the courtroom froze for a moment, taking in what had just happened. A couple of the jury's eyes widened, and it was not a good start for Uncle! He sat in his usual way manner: back straight, chest out, legs apart, one hand on his knee {occasionally slapping it), and the other hand on the desk in front of him. He looked confident and not at all flustered; quite the opposite of me during my stint in the witness box. I had barely been able to hold things together.

"So," the barrister went on to say, "what surrounded the events on that day when Pippa, at six years old, came to stay with you and you took a phone call?" The story unfolded, and Rob and Ann were fascinated to hear his version of events.

His narrative put all the blame on me as a six-year-old, saying that I had stroked his legs and gone too high, so he had brushed me off angrily as he was tense whilst waiting for a very important phone call, and my attention had rattled him. He explained that he had then gone to answer the call, had sat on the stairs, and I had run up to him in my sandals and clumsily stumbled over his foot, pulling off his toenail. According to him, this had all happened whilst he was sorting out an issue for work, which was a big job involving lots of lorries. He described the problem in intricate detail!

How on earth could he remember that one job in that much detail, forty-eight years later? This was something he did daily: organising men and machinery...but how could he remember such an insignificant event unless it was during a significant event? For me, remembering that event from forty-eight years ago was different as it was a life-changing moment and imprinted in my memory. How could I forget him talking on the phone to Stanley whilst he was sexually assaulting me? His account sounded ludicrous and inadequate, yet he remained confident and unruffled as he continued to be cross-examined.

The defence barrister asked, "So Ivan, did you help out at home? Did you bath the children and help with the cooking?"

The way in which he answered the question was quite shocking and revelatory of his character. He sounded bigoted and full of disdain for what he described as being *'her job'*. He scoffed at the idea, appearing to find it ridiculous and beneath him which, in turn, showed him to be far from a kind, helpful dad and uncle. As he was pressed on these issues, he showed nothing but contempt for the idea of helping out at home, which came back to bite him when it was later pointed out that if he did not bath his own children, why would he bath me or be involved in creaming my eczema.

There were several questions that his own barrister put to him that Uncle Ivan surprised everyone by answering in a way that his barrister had not wanted or expected, which really didn't do him any favours.

Moving on through the questions, he was asked if he could remember an incident when I was fourteen concerning the downstairs toilet room. He said that he could and that he remembered knocking on the door as someone was inside.

"What time of day was this?" asked the barrister.

"It was in the morning. I remember it was breakfast time as I had a bowl of cereal in my hand," said Uncle Ivan.

In my ABE interview, I had described it as being late at night. It was dark, and everyone had been asleep. I had needed the bathroom and, because someone was in the upstairs one, I had gone to the downstairs toilet room. Uncle Ivan *had* knocked. In fact, it was an unrelenting and determined knock, and I had felt pressured, with no choice but to eventually open the door. There he had stood with his penis out, and another one of his assaults had then taken place.

A little further on, the barrister repeated his question to Uncle and asked for the time of day again. "It was around lunchtime," he said, without realising that he had just contradicted himself.

It was becoming more and more evident that Uncle was possibly approaching his demise when he went onto to deliver yet another inaccuracy. After a few sentences, the barrister cleverly asked one final time for the clarification on the time of day he had knocked on the door. This time, Uncle said he thought it had been around the evening time. Whether in this very short space of time it was his nerves, the pressure, or getting muddled up with his lies that had caused Uncle Ivan to have a lapse of memory, he had certainly undermined his case and reinforced mine.

By the time his cross-examination had come to an end, the judge asked his barrister if he had anything to add. He answered, "No, Judge." By this time, he had his hands on his head and his elbows on the desk and, in despondency, didn't even look up at the judge.

The unusual and surprising thing was that Uncle Ivan did not refute that he had been on holiday either time with me, and he had remembered each time I had said he was with me (although denied the assaults being part of them). So, in essence, he placed himself at the scene of every crime which seemed an unusual stance to take.

During his whole cross examination, Uncle Ivan did not show any sign that he thought he was defeated but instead maintained his demeanour, appearing composed and unperturbed. He simply refuted everything and said that none of the sexual encounters had happened.

Rob and Ann saw his barrister walking through the hallway, after that afternoon's revelations and ordeal, with his wig in his hand and looking rather dejected. His client had certainly not made his case very easy to navigate or prove in court. Not only that, but there also had not been even one witness for the defence other than the defendant, my uncle.

Whilst all this was happening down the road in court, I was having my own difficulties back at the hotel. I had stayed in the room all day as I felt unsettled and anxious. As the day wore on, I got into a state emotionally and felt sick, just like when I had been in the dock. The situation was overwhelming me. I felt I couldn't ring Geoff as he was on his way home and I did not want him to be in a predicament, wondering whether he should turn round and drive all the way back to Scotland. I wanted Sophia because she understood trauma and probably would know exactly what I was experiencing, but she and Dan had done so much for me during the build up to the trial and going into court for three days.

Rob and Ann could not have their phones on in court, plus they couldn't just stand up and leave, so although I was desperate to see them and needed them, I knew that was not happening either. I couldn't keep my eyes open, and my face went stone cold. I started to tremble and shake, my arms and legs went freezing cold, and I could not think straight. My heart was pounding, and I paced the floor for several hours. It felt like my brain and emotions were having a breakdown. I could not stop rambling to myself and found that the words weren't coming out right.

In this dishevelled, desperate state, I rang my friend Sara who I really had not wanted to disturb as she'd just given birth. She would do anything for me, but she felt limited as her baby was born a week before the trial started. She had bought me some Chanel to wear during the trial so every time I had a whiff of scent, I would be reminded that she would be thinking of and praying for me. Sara understands trauma as she is a councillor too and, within a short time, she had helped to calm me a little.

Giving in, I rang Sophia, who agreed with Sara; I was in shock. They were so far away which made it hard for them as all they could do was give me advice on how to stay safe and warm and hydrated. I curled up in bed and waited for Rob and Ann to return from court. I don't remember much about what happened once they arrived back to the hotel. All I do remember is that I needed a drink: an alcoholic one, and a big one at that. As much as I hated this, it had become a coping mechanism, and it helped in the moment.

I felt so guilty that I had all these people in my life who I needed. I was ashamed and regretful that I had reached my fifties and still needed encouragement, comfort and understanding. God, in His love and wisdom, had provided them for this time and they all assured me they wouldn't wish to be anywhere else.

I set off for home with Rob and Ann but can't remember much of the journey. It felt so wrong to leave Scotland as the trial was still in progress, yet there was absolutely nothing I could achieve by staying. Leaving Scotland felt like I had left unfinished business, but I knew that if he was found guilty, I would be returning in a few weeks for sentencing.

There it was…that '**if**' word. There were so many uncertainties and all I could do now was wait again. I went to stay with Ann as going home felt like the wrong place to be. How could I be in my normal everyday environment when the most horrendous thing was taking place, and I felt I couldn't be the wife and Mum at home. I needed to be looked after and given space to be whatever I needed to be. I was not sure what that would look like but, for once, it wasn't about anyone else; it was only about me.

The chaos in my mind raged and the first night was horrific. As I started to cry and sobbed loudly from the pit of my stomach, I felt bereft, broken, desolate, grief stricken and alone. I wasn't alone, though. Ann was with me and Rob was not far away, I felt small again and just wanted to be held and be told that I did not have to do anything or be anything. Ann and Rob gave me everything I needed but my heart was so alone. It felt impermeable and so fragmented. I don't really remember going to bed that night, but I woke in the early hours, beside myself with anxiety. I was shaking and confused, feeling separate from my surroundings as though I was part of another world. I stared at the tray of things Ann had so meticulously loaded with everything possible any guest could ever want, covering every eventuality and need, a hundred notches up from hotel amenities.

"What should I do? I don't know what to do! Please help me! Everyone's going to be so angry! I'm sorry, I'm so sorry! Please forgive me! I don't know what to do!"

In a rambling state, I repeated these statements. I didn't know who I was talking to, but I just could not stop. Over and over again, I repeated the words, not able to calm myself or pray.

Today was Friday and it was 02.00. In seven hours, Court 4 would be opening its doors and everyone in every capacity for the trial would be there, waiting for summing up to begin! I was sick at the thought of it. If only I knew what they were summing up. How well had Uncle Ivan done and how inadequately had I performed? I could not allow myself to believe it to be the other way around.

There, in the dead of night, I rang Carl, the husband of Anna who had been one of my witnesses. Carl had a history of working in mental health and social care and had worked for Mencap. He listened and talked in such a way that I felt understood. Unbeknown to me, he was really concerned, yet he managed to stay calm and get some sense into me so that I could eventually fall asleep. Carl had been in court and had watched the trauma I went through during my three hours of cross-examination.

Friday passed in a blur. I couldn't eat and could not rest. Finally, DC Gallucci called me.

"Pippa, summing up is complete. All we can do now is wait for the Jury's decision."

I wanted an indication that it was going well for me and needed reassurance, but I had been on the criminal justice journey too long to know that there are no guarantees and often surprises along the way. One thing was a fact: no more could be said or done. For the jury, what a sobering thought-provoking weekend they were sure to have, waiting for Monday: trial day number seven and hopefully 'Verdict Day'!

The jury (my angels) had sat through the worst unfolding story, and they had remained focused. Over the course of the trial, they were seen to be shocked, tearful and clearly moved by the evidence that had been presented to them. It was now all in their hands.

## Chapter Twenty

## The Verdict

The public gallery split clearly into two halves. Uncle Ivan's side of the family had occupied the left-hand side all week during the trial. Their positions changed as the trial progressed, but Auntie Glenda remained on the front row.

The day before 'Verdict Day' my children suddenly realised, before I did, that no one was representing me in court and that absolutely no one would be sitting on our side on the most important day of it all. WHY? They could not bear it, and, between themselves, they hatched a plan. It was well on the way before I got wind of it.

Joy and Lewis drove to Cambridge to pick up Belle, who had moved there the week before. It was a long drive after work for them all but absolutely nothing was going to stop their mission, and they were on their way to Scotland.

Initially, I cringed at the thought of them knowing exactly what Uncle Ivan had done to me; it felt wrong, not to mention utterly embarrassing! I felt ashamed as I knew all the charges would be mentioned and it made me recoil with horror to think of the detail the judge would go into in his final summing up. I had not told my children everything as I'd tried to protect them from the details. However, as time went on, I resigned myself to the idea of them knowing, and actually felt something lift off me; it was another layer of shame.

It felt releasing, and the people I loved the most in the world would actually know the level of pain I had endured as a little girl. Maybe they would understand a bit more why I am often paralysed with insecurities!

They were adults, and they all needed to stand and defend their Mum. They needed to fortify their utter defence and unity of me. How could I deny them that?

They arrived at the grotty mossy-green hotel, where we had all encountered the tables that were that constantly sticky. If anything was loose on your person, it would have been left behind!

Once settled in the court room, Joy, Lewis and Belle couldn't believe the intensity and magnitude of what they had walked into. They were about to encounter a momentous decision, and the atmosphere was thick with tension. Lewis' face was twitching like he'd never encountered before, and Joy squeezed her eyes shut and did not dare open them; she couldn't allow herself to look at the jury as they walked in, fearing that what they were to about to deliver might be the news she was dreading... a 'not guilty' verdict!

Belle sat rigid, unable to take her eyes off 'the other side'. Her defence barriers were up and at their limit; she was not going to let any of them off with anything if they put a foot out of line. In that moment, they were all there in utter defence of me whilst feeling overwhelmed with pride of how far I had come and what I had achieved.

The jury reached their decision by mid-afternoon on Monday. Whilst they went through each offence and delivered their guilty verdict on each, Uncle Ivan didn't appear to react until the 'guiltys' were mounting up. Until this point, he had remained calm and seemingly unaffected.

Once the juror had delivered the final 'guilty' blow to Uncle Ivan, the judge turned all his attention towards him and, with a firm and weighty tone in his voice, said, "You have been found guilty of all nine offences, and these are serious offences. You will face an immediate and substantial prison term at sentencing." Uncle Ivan suddenly started to react as his whole body-language changed. His neck jerked and he looked out of his depth as the seriousness and alarm of the situation appeared to be finally sinking in.

DC Gallucci rang me, and I saw *Caller withheld*. I was petrified! I was sitting with Rob and Ann and said, "This is it! I'm scared to answer!" I squirmed and jumped to my feet, unable to be still. I couldn't answer immediately, despite it being the call for which I'd lived and breathed. Holy Spirit help!

"Hello," I said with trepidation.

"Hello, Pippa," DC Gallucci said in his calm manner. There was no hanging back...he launched straight into the result. "Pippa, he's been found **guilty** of rape of a minor and **all** eight other sexual offences. It's a great result! You did it! You **WON!**"

GUILTY ON ALL NINE COUNTS!

Rape of a female under 16
Indecent assault of a girl under the age of 16 years
Indecent assault of a girl under the age of 16 years
Indecent assault of a girl under the age of 16 years
Indecent assault of a girl under the age of 14 years
Indecent assault of a girl under the age of 14 years
Indecent assault of a girl under the age of 14 years
Indecent assault of a girl under the age of 14 years
Indecent assault of a girl under the age of 14 years

I did my best to thank DC Gallucci; I had already rehearsed a heartfelt thanks, but it all went out of the window. My brain could not take it all in and I felt stunned. "Guilty. He's guilty!" I repeated it over and over again. In fact, I repeated it under my breath for about a week as I couldn't get it to sink in.

DC Gallucci explained that Uncle Ivan had been sent home on bail to put his affairs in order. He had six weeks.

He went on to describe what the judge had said: he had spoken to Uncle directly and firmly explained that he had been found guilty of rape and eight other sexual offences and that these were very serious crimes. He had gone on to say, "Because of this, I am letting you go home to put your affairs in order because when you come back at sentencing, you will be given an immediate and substantial sentence." I was aghast, and it all felt surreal.

"Pippa, this will probably be in the paper too, so don't be surprised," said DC Gallucci calmly, although I could detect an air of achievement in his voice. "In six weeks, the waiting will finally be over. Well done! Pippa, you did it!"

I knew at this point that the kids would have rung Geoff. It was our agreement that they would tell him the minute they got out of the court room. Jenny was one of the first people I told as she was my closest cousin and had truly supported me and understood all my reasonings behind my decisions. She shrilled with joy, and we cried together. It was unbelievable to think that all those years ago, she was actually under the same roof when it was all happening, yet she knew nothing. But here today, we both emotionally shared the joy and relief that our Uncle Ivan had finally been faced with what he had done, and he was now going to have to pay the consequences of his crimes.

However, over the next few days, shell shock set in and I was consumed by conflicting thoughts. I wanted to stay out of circulation forever! While hiding away, I would not have to explain anything or reshape my emotions to fit other people's expectations.

I couldn't shake off the intense notion that I had gravely brought ruination to my mum's sister. How unbelievably selfish had I been, just to be heard. "Well, was it worth it?" I reprimanded myself.

All I could see in front of me was a pile of wreckage. Every single person involved had some level of damage as a result of what they had just gone through. All because I opened my mouth. There were no winners, and everyone had lost something. Whatever side we were on, we had all fought with all our might. I had fought for the truth to be heard, and Uncle Ivan had fought for his freedom and to keep his good name intact.

Whilst the battles were raging in court with clever words from the barristers, another higher, more profound battle was raging. The battle between the Kingdom of light and darkness. The little girl who grew up nurturing a relationship with Jesus shone a beacon of light wherever she went, and that sort of light cannot be overshadowed by darkness. The seal of God's love and approval was on my life. I had given Him my heart as a little girl and, from an early age, I knew that the same love of Jesus that drew me to Him was available to everyone, and I made it my mission to share it.

When the enemy of my soul, Satan, had seen this, he had thrown every grenade he could into my life to knock me off course, and the worst of all the attempts was to destroy my identity through sexual abuse. He had not wanted me to signpost others into their true identity. Oh yes, those bombs went off. Bits of me were blown off and damaged, but every wound the enemy inflicted, Jesus had already borne it on the cross for me. Who, of themselves, can forgive when you're hurt repeatedly and brutally? Who can love when your love has been abused and trampled on? Who can trust when your trust has been exploited? And who can show fairness when they have been treated with depravity and filth?

*No one can but Jesus.*

Jesus became my identity the moment I invited Him into my heart. It is Him in me that can forgive, that can love and can still trust and be kind and fair. When God lives on the inside of a person, their spirit grows and takes on God's way of thinking, and the world views weaken as God's heart increases. So, when in court I was asked about forgiveness, the biggest of all grenades was thrown back into the kingdom of darkness and it delivered a damning blow.

The enemy of our souls can do a good job, but only God can do a complete job. What the enemy used to harm me, God had already in his foreknowledge planned and weaved great hope for me and a future. Uncle Ivan did not have this, and his life had not been seeking after God.

To any onlooker, the war appeared one-sided but, oh, the damage! Layer upon layer, year after year, Uncle Ivan had lived his life without God, fulfilling his own dreams and evil desires and became more lost. His own evilness had caught up with him and he was ensnared. God was my saving defence in court that day, and the years of abuse and trauma were exposed for what they were. The light shone in the darkness and had overshadowed it.

## Chapter Twenty-One

## Sentencing

*Six whole weeks to wait!*

Did I feel victorious? Did I feel that I had won? No, I didn't. I felt overwhelmed with grief and guilt.

The first night, Ann and Rob took me to Dan and Sophia's, where they all united in trying to help me to hold together my shattered world, and Ann had stayed up all night, holding my hand. Julie ramped up her phone calls, and Team Pippa were running a relay race to get me to the finishing line. I felt so unbelievably tired and done with it all, yet I knew the final day was coming and it would all be complete. But what was I to do after that? What would become of the inner child that still felt deep sadness? It felt as if everyone was expecting me to miraculously grow up, which would leave the child in me alone and abandoned. I had an air of panic in my heart every time I thought of it.

The renewing of my mind had to start from the point where my inner child had been hurt. I knew the Holy Spirit wanted to soothe and put my crippled heart back together from that point. That journey had begun but, without an instantaneous miracle, it would take time and lots of patience. I felt very scared that the little girl would be forgotten when she still needed more help and attention.

The expectation and pressure I felt was intense and was part of why I just wanted to hide away and do nothing. The trauma of the trial was still very much with me, and I'd had no real time to process it before I was thrust into the preparation for sentencing.

I run my home like a ship and love everything in its place. A big 'clear out' is like my birthday and Christmas all rolled into one. I am so organised and love every item to have its place. I pride myself in knowing where the most obscure items are at any given time. None of this hunting for Sellotape or 25-watt screw cap bulbs! Everything has its place. However, I ashamedly admit that during this time, I threw things out that didn't need to go. I had an insatiable need to order things externally because, internally, my mind was in chaos.

Gradually, though, I slipped into a period of finding myself unmotivated, wanting to stay in bed and not really caring whether I cleaned up or not. This all came as a shock. I had never seen so much dust on my surfaces and scum round my bathtub. As I look back now, it feels like a blur and a time in my life where my past felt as confusing as the present. The future seemed just as confusing, and my mantra was, "I'm just so mixed up!" I could not articulate or try to overcome something that I couldn't fathom.

I relied on the fact that Jesus knew it all, and I had no choice but to leave it with Him and just accept that I was 'mixed up'. "It's fine to not understand something that doesn't make sense!" was Sophia's one liner. It was all held in God's wisdom and timing.

Rob and Ann could not join me for the sentencing which was a blow to me. Ann was gutted. They had got me this far, amazingly, always been there and knew everything. I felt like a lifeline had been ripped away and the old feelings of abandonment tried to take root. By God's grace, I accepted that He had provided me with their great care and now had seamlessly provided Dan and Sophia to lean heavier on for the sentencing.

It was Friday, and the dirty mossy-green hotel was booked. We waited anxiously for the call to come from the CPS to tell us that it was on. Sentencing was due to go ahead on the Monday.

The call came from Julie. "Now, Pippa," she said, followed by a long pause. "Firstly, it *is* on." There was another long pause. I sensed something was wrong, and my insides dropped like a brick.

She explained that the judge was residing and overseeing his cases in a different part of Scotland to where the trial had taken place, but he didn't want to adjourn my case either. Julie went on to explain that if I would be willing to travel to him for the sentencing, he would let it go ahead. I agreed and sighed in relief but sensed there was more news coming.

"Pippa, I can't make it to this part of Scotland to support you." I felt another blow. Julie had been my rock in advocating for me with the police and helping me to understand during one of the most stressful events anyone can go through: a Crown Court process. She had fought for me and believed in me and now Rob, Ann and Julie wouldn't be there!

The court and the police believed this event could have the potential to be highly volatile as Auntie Glenda was emotionally unstable and she had acted unpredictably during the trial. Therefore, the general consensus was that it would be in everyone's best interests to keep my supporters in court to a minimum. So, I had four supporters in court: Dan, Sophia, Joy and Lewis. Julie said that four was more than enough in this situation.

Shona, the ISVA that had jumped in to support me for the first trial that had been adjourned, came flying to my aid. Shona and Julie were a formidable force. They both fiercely and wholeheartedly supported their clients with no fear of upsetting the higher powers, using their tenacity, expertise and humour to get what they wanted when and where they wanted it. They were amazing women and I was incredibly blessed to have had their help when I needed it. So, Julie handed my care over to Shona for the sentencing. I accepted it, and Dan, Sophia and I were on our way to Scotland for the last time.

We had to drive so near the house where the abuse had happened, and I wanted Dan and Sophia to see it, just like Ann had all those months before. We sat outside, and I pointed to each window again as I explained to them what had happened in those rooms. This was the last time I would ever stand where I had cried and cowered away, trying to stay safe! My pastors stood with me, and we all nodded and looked at each other with sobering thoughts and said, "Let's go!"

That was it! It was done! I silently asked the Holy Spirit to heal me and use this visit to move me forward and away from the past.

The morning of Uncle Ivan's sentencing had arrived, and I did my usual final check in the mirror before I left my hotel room. I didn't feel as smart or 'together' as I had the other times. All I needed was to just get there and survive it.

This was it! In a short while, I was, for the first time in a few years, going to stand facing Uncle Ivan, the man who'd had such an invisible and invincible control over me. This time, there would be no special measures and no screens. Just faces. Faces I was dreading seeing. What on earth would we both think of each other? What would he look like? It had been six months since DC Gallucci had inadvertently walked me straight past him. He was in a different position then...accused but not convicted...but today he was being presented as a convicted rapist and paedophile.

Would I be shocked by his appearance? Would his eyes bore into me with anger? I felt as if I was the guilty one, and everyone on the left-hand side of the public gallery was sure to act out that very notion, with their comments and disturbing body language towards me.

We waited as the clock ticked on, and court was finally in session. Dan, Sophia, Shona and I sat in a rather grand room with a library of law books that were meticulously stacked to the ceiling. I paced, chewing my copious amounts of gum. "There we go," I said to myself as the burping began! I had nerves upon nerves. Joy and Lewis had gone through the front doors and into court to be present from the onset, and I wondered how they were.

The heavy, dark oak door opened slowly, and the CPS official came calmly round it and said, "It's time to go in, Pippa."

"Here we go again!" I thought to myself.

Apparently, no gum was allowed in court, but no one had told me. I chewed and swallowed and burped for England, but somehow, no one caught sight of it or challenged me, thank goodness, although Sophia had been challenged over her Fruit Pastilles!

I looked frantically at Dan and Sophia. If ever looks could give you strength, they willed them to me in bucket-loads! "Come on; you can do this!" they both said, and we walked into court together.

Suddenly, as I started walking, my peripheral vision disappeared and nor could I hear as clearly. I felt as though I was walking in a mist, with everything appearing in slow motion. There seemed to be an entourage around me as if I was being bundled along the corridor.

As I stepped into the courtroom, I was acutely aware of the presence of my uncle's immediate family to my left, only a few steps away. I glanced over quickly. Oh goodness! Who was there?

Before I could grasp what was happening, I was walked straight to the witness box, not computing that I would be the first up. Fumbling to get my bearings, I tried to adjust the chair to get closer to the microphone but caught it on the carpet and it wouldn't move. I was stressed beyond words.

It was time to read my personal statement in which I had not only talked about how Uncle Ivan's actions had affected me since the dreadful events in my childhood, but also referred to Auntie Glenda by saying how sorry I was for the pain that she was suffering. However, just beforehand, my barrister had warned me that I may be pulled up on my references to Auntie Glenda as she was not part of the criminal proceedings.

I turned to speak to the judge to clarify what part of my statement I ought not to be reading out, but had forgotten, under the pressure, that no one addresses the judge unless they are given permission. In that moment, I needed reassurance and, fortunately, the judge responded graciously and just said, "Go ahead."

I finally managed to get close enough to the microphone and looked across at Uncle Ivan in his toughened glass box. He looked old and small, and his skin looked grey. For the first time in years, Uncle Ivan was not wearing his thick dark sunglasses, and he stared straight at me, despite being registered as blind, without wavering his gaze. I felt a mixture of repulsion and fear, and the old guilt whispered, "What have you done!"

He didn't blink, move, or react at all during my Victim Personal Statement. I read it with intense feeling. It was not just for him but for Auntie Glenda too. I wanted both of them, and my cousins, to get a real understanding of what Uncle Ivan's moments of gratification had done to my young mind, personality and body. I desperately needed them to see how it had permeated every part of my life. Maybe, just maybe something would click, and Uncle Ivan would actually listen and see the gravity of the damage he had caused.

He gave nothing away. Not a flicker. Julie had repeatedly warned me that when paedophiles get to the point of sentencing without showing any remorse, it is an indication that nothing will change. He was in denial of his guilt, and it appeared that Auntie Glenda was too.

My statement was about twenty minutes long and, throughout it, Auntie Glenda gasped and poured utter disgust and derision on the things I was saying by making gasping, groaning and tutting noises, muttering disdainful things about me, calling me a wicked woman and a liar. Her attitude towards me was of utter contempt.

I had forgotten that Joy and Lewis were present and, as I caught sight of them, I wondered what on earth they must have been thinking and feeling. No mother wants their kids to hear shocking explanations of the pain they have gone through; it's Mum's job to be the rock and glue of the family.

But I had done it! Yes, I had cried and had to take several pauses, but finally, after forty-eight years, I had used my words to tell Uncle Ivan exactly what he had done.

Leaving the witness box, I was guided past the glass box and looked in Uncle's eyes as I passed. It took me back to those times when his eyes were an inch away from mine and all the times that he had intimidated me by insisting nothing was going to stop him. Today, they looked blank and emotionless. He didn't look as if he were even present.

Astonishingly, I was walked across the courtroom right in front of Auntie Glenda, Uncle Ivan's grandchildren, Stanley and others. I didn't know where to look! I could see Auntie hanging over the rails, a mixture of being utterly distressed, angry and shocked, as if the worst thing in the world had become part of her world...and it had.

In a split nanosecond, I prayed and chose to look up into her face as I passed by. I had the thought that this may be the last time I would ever look into the face of the auntie I loved. Her eyes looked intently into mine for a moment. If only I could have spoken to her! But what words could ever convey the gravity of what I genuinely felt. I saw her feeling of being betrayed; she looked hurt beyond words. Her face said, "How could you!" It was angry and swollen, with tears rolling down her cheeks. My heart felt like it was going to explode with anguish. I felt her pain, but there wasn't a flicker of acknowledgment that she felt even one moment of mine.

As I walked along the front row, Uncle Ivan's granddaughter rolled her eyes and looked outraged. Oh, my heart broke at that. She was the same age as Belle and, for the rest of her life, she would carry the awful burden that her grandad was a convicted paedophile. She would probably live in the denial of that, trying to convince herself and those around of his innocence.

The repercussions of sin cascade through the generations, and it is only Jesus that can cut us free from the chains that this bondage brings. Just as children who are adopted take on a new birthright, the same is true of anyone who turns to Jesus; He breaks the power of the sin, there and then, as he has cancelled it out by his death on the cross.

My heart's prayer for Auntie's future generations, just like mine, is that they are set free from the repercussions and bondages that sexual sin brings. The beginning of that is to acknowledge the truth and put right the part that any of us played in it.

I stumbled into my seat and sat between Dan and Sophia. They grabbed my hands and held them all the way through to the end. Dan sat between me and the other side. It felt the safest positioning. The court officials stood nearby and were constantly assessing the room, ready to act if needed.

The judge began.

The room was poised with tension and anticipation. My knuckles were white, and poor Dan and Sophia's hands must have been throbbing. Unfortunately, the big glass box that housed Uncle Ivan and his guards was positioned centrally in the room. This not only made it hard to see round it, but also muffled the sound, creating a two-fold difficulty. Not only was it difficult to fully hear everything the judge saying, but the judge did not hear the noises and comments the other side were making towards me either.

They'd already had to be removed from court during the trial in order to be reprimanded by the defence barrister and were warned that they must not speak or make a sound otherwise they would be removed from court permanently. On this day, though, they got away with it.

I slumped down in my chair and, looking to my left under the protection of Dan's chin, I looked at Auntie. She was hanging over the rail, dishevelled and with a wild look. She did not take her eyes off me and audibly mouthed, "Wicked! So wicked!" I could not comprehend the extreme reaction as I knew that she knew in her heart of hearts that he was guilty. I had told her twenty years before that Uncle Ivan had touched me. On that night, I knew that she believed me, but she could not bear the ramifications and consequences of the facts. It was easier to blame me.

The judge was serious and very firm as he began to lay out the reasoning behind his decision and referred to the laws that he had to consider in order to bring him to his conclusion on the length of the sentence. He unapologetically explained that he would not be doing the right thing if he did not help the court to see the seriousness of Uncle Ivan's crimes, which required the appropriate length of sentence to match their severity.

"Pippa was six years old, and you penetrated her vagina. She was alone, away from home and vulnerable. You and your wife should have protected her; after all, you were her uncle. You caused her pain as you went on to do several sexual acts, escalating and repeating them. I am reflecting these in the length of sentence I'm about to give you."

I wanted to disappear. I wanted to scream and, above anything, run. I was ashamed and aghast! Yes, all these things had been unravelled during the trial, but I had not expected them to be so explicitly uttered here. Plus, my ears had not heard them said in court as the defence barrister had questioned me more on the environment and occasions of the crimes, rather than the crimes themselves. The acts had been talked about whilst I was not in the room, much to my relief.

He continued to stress the seriousness of his crimes and the abhorrent nature of them. I have written about these in my first book, after deliberating over their distastefulness and whether or not they should be included. Everything in me has struggled to write about them, but I want the reader to feel a bit of the reaction that the judge's statement caused in me. That little girl...me...represents millions.

The reality is that this is happening all over the world, in every walk of life, class, religious group and amongst every people group.

The judge continued to explain that the law at the time of the offences had to be applied. He said that he was doing it with regret as he would want to give Uncle Ivan the maximum sentence that today's law would impose...which he added could be between twenty-two to thirty years.

But his hands were tied, and, with obvious regret, he said that he would be giving him a shorter sentence than he would like, but the maximum possible by law.

The judge thanked me for my Victim Personal Statement and said it was read with eloquence and great impact. He said that it was very clear to see the devastating impact Ivan's crimes had placed on me.

The sound of the judge's voice was muffled at times, and I didn't manage to hear everything, but I did hear the sentence as it was delivered.

As I write this right now, I am moved again. At that moment, I felt heard, defended and valued as that six-year-old and young teenager. All the years of pain had been acknowledged and laid bare, and action was about to be taken.

Uncle Ivan was given fourteen years in prison and should serve just over nine of them. He was eighty-six years of age, so the chances are that he will never go home.

He stood to his feet and his arms flared, and he was immediately made to sit back down by the guards.

Auntie Glenda gasped, and the tension in the room was tangible. I was shaking, by this point, and my face, nose, hands and legs had again gone stone cold. The judge concluded and asked the court to rise. It was a heart-pounding moment, and it felt like time stood still as the guards were told to take him away.

Uncle Ivan was walked past me, along the glass walkway. He shuffled so slowly; his face still blank. Auntie Glenda shouted at the judge, "Can I kiss him?" and then shouted to Uncle, "I love you, Ivan!" There was a commotion as the guards jumped up to block her because she desperately wanted to get to him, but it was to no avail as the court officials kept everyone in their place.

Once he had left the room, the court officials, Dan and Sophia bundled me out again as fast as possible, with Joy and Lewis close behind. I looked back at Auntie, shocked at her total lack of care for me. As I left the court, she lunged towards me and shouted, "Liar, Liar!" I was grief-stricken. I ran out and fell against the wall, my legs barely able to carry me, but my entourage kept me moving as fast as they could to get me away from 'the other side'.

The next part was a blur, but I remember going to the toilet. I was alone and as I stood empty, staring at the taps, the window open, I could hear Auntie; she was crying hysterically. I pushed my arms out of the window as if I was reaching for her to touch her. I was so deeply sad and distressed for both of us. I knew I would most probably never be able to be close to her again.

## Chapter Twenty-Two

## The Grey Van

*Where were they taking Uncle Ivan?*

I felt churned up and sick to the pit of my stomach as I started to walk out of court. He was not only convicted, but he was also, today, starting to pay the price of what he had done. In 2038, his crimes would be paid for in full. It felt surreal!

Was he in a cell downstairs waiting, or had he been taken straight into the van to wait collectively, as some prisoners are? I guess the reality of this had not ever fully crossed my mind. The horror of the situation for him, for Auntie Glenda and my cousins hit me. We turned the corner of the building, and I froze solid to the spot. The van! It was huge, with small windows along the top, dark grey and imposing.

"Nooooo! Is he in there? Oh no! He's in there! I'm sorry; so sorry! What have I done? Uncle Ivan, I'm sorry!" Faced with the reality of what I saw before me, my feelings tumbled out of me with grief-stricken, misguided ramblings. Tears poured down my face and I felt utterly lost in the moment. I had no idea whether he was in there. If not, it was inevitably where he was heading.

When trauma is involved, although one can previously feel that something is dealt with and settled, when finding ourselves in different or challenging circumstances, the thing we thought had been sorted can hit us out of the blue. I thought I had dealt with the fact that Uncle Ivan had found himself in this position because of his choices and not because of anything I had done wrong. But here I was, utterly crushed again under the guilt of my decision to report him. In front of my very eyes, I was facing the unchangeable fact that he was soon going to be driven away as a convict, losing his life and freedom.

It took many more months to adjust to the fact that I wasn't guilty and that I was not responsible for where Uncle Ivan had found himself. However, the old feelings of guilt still revisit and have to be challenged from time-to-time.

The guilt we carry, any sort of guilt, can sometimes feel like we are unable to lift it off ourselves, regardless of the help and encouragement we receive and the truth we hear and know. Jesus carried ALL mankind's guilt: real guilt and misaligned guilt, the guilt placed on us by our own sin, and guilt laid on us by a perpetrator. He carried it all.

The beautiful thing about Jesus is that where we fall short, he makes up the shortfall thoroughly and completely. All he requires is for us to believe it and hand it over. You might only need to hand it over once, but in my case and for many who have suffered sexual abuse, it must be repeatedly handed over and put where it belongs as only Jesus is strong enough to bear it. The renewing of the mind is a rehabilitation and reconstruction. The transformation that Jesus brings is sometimes instant but in most cases of abuse and trauma, it takes the gentle and guiding hand of God to bring about the change over time and with our cooperation.

As I stood staring at the van, Dan and Sophia got hold of me from each side to try and walk me forward, but I was rooted to the spot. How could I just walk on into my life, as if Uncle Ivan being taken away in a van was just a normal everyday course of action...as if it shouldn't matter. But it did matter!

This was the end of the road of my responsibility in the criminal process. It was over. He was being taken away for heinous and abhorrent crimes, yet as I started to walk away from court, I still felt like that little girl who could not escape this nightmare, and I somehow felt responsible.

I stood, suddenly solid to the spot, feeling every bit of it. Eventually, after repeatedly saying how sorry I was, we started to edge slowly forward, my neck craned as I obsessed over the van. The walk past seemed endless, and my legs gave way with the trauma of it all. Dan and Sophia scooped me up, and finally got me back to the car, just about in one piece. It was done!

JUSTICE HAD BEEN SERVED!

And I had survived!

The three of us set off, shell-shocked. What had just happened? It was a lot to get my head around: the tense serious atmosphere in court, that we had moments ago come out of; Uncle Ivan in a glass box, emotionless; the judge in his weighty sentencing capacity; Uncle Ivan's family at their wits' end with grief, anger and probably total disbelief; the reading of my Victim Personal Statement; my added emotion of reliving every detail the judge had gone through; my children holding a complexity of extreme emotions...and all under one roof, all at the same time.

Everyone had invested everything they had into the trial, as each person's future rested on the outcome. This was a day, I'm sure, that no one who was in court would ever forget.

Starting the car, we left Scotland behind for the very last time.

Just like after the trial itself, I could not bear to go home again and get on with normal life as I needed a buffer and time to recover.

Dan and Sophia delivered me to Carl and Anna's for a few days' care and recuperation. Finally, I could catch up with Anna. She had been one of my witnesses and we had not been able to speak about the case before but, now it was over, I would be able to talk freely about the part she had played in court. Carl's mental health training and understanding of trauma and Anna's kindness and constant reassurance were perfect.

Albeit the next few days were far from smooth emotionally, and my coping mechanisms were in full swing, I scraped through and survived! It was tough because I had no idea what to do with the feelings I was experiencing as I didn't understand them. The guilt, the shame, the void, the fear of expectation and then back round again to the guilt and so on, in a vicious circle.

This was the beginning of the rest of my life, but the future scared me as I struggled to know the way forward from this point.

I had a huge void, but it felt like a black hole. I had fought all my life and now I'd had the fight removed. Up until then, the relationships with the police and the ISVAs (Julie and Shona) had felt intense and were, in a sense, holding me up. But now it was over, I thought they were gone, and I was being expected to move on by myself. But what to? I felt a huge sense of loss and grief.

Everyone had their opinions, but how could they really understand? Even though the criminal justice process was over, I still had to live with me and the residue of a long, exhausting internal battle. Just because the decisions had been made in a day, it did not mean that I would change overnight.

Sophia and Julie constantly reminded me that it was completely normal to feel lost. I did for a long time. However, I was blessed...Julie was still available for me until I no longer needed her.

I learned to ride the waves: difficult days, traumatic days, slightly better days, and everything in between. My mum's words, although she had gone, teamed up with Sophia's, having shared exactly the same view: "IT WILL PASS!" Tomorrow is always a new day, and God's mercies are new every morning.

This is the hardest part of my book to write...the ending. I guess it's because there is no clear-cut ending for me.

My story has been told. Its pain and its sadness have been heard. It has now been written about in two books and there was a just and fair trial and conclusion to Uncle Ivan and Jerry's prosecutions.

I want to be able to say to you, after this long journey that I have been on and that you have followed as you've read my books, that I am free. But here's the truth: I am not there yet but am being renewed every day, bit by bit, choice by choice and, believe me, it is the best way forward.

It's kind, gentle, and all in God's timing. There's only one opinion that really counts to me on how well I'm progressing. I have spent my life pleasing others, but now my only objective is to please the One.

Underpinning my existence and fortifying me is Jesus. His opinion is unrivalled.

He was there at my conception and saw my birth. He held my heart and stored up my tears in His bottle when no one else saw them fall, and in Heaven is a record of every single one. Not one was shed without His knowledge or grievance.

Sexual abuse isolates the soul and the individual, but the gentle love of Jesus uses everything to draw us near to Himself. I have a heart like many of yours; it's sectioned off, parts totally padlocked and other parts dead and present but with no feeling.

Trust is a gigantic deal. It can be shattered a thousand ways but the One who formed me has only one objective: to restore my heart to function in full capacity. I am learning to let go and surrender every part.

As I sit in my lounge writing this, Uncle Ivan has been in prison for four months.

I am still very aware of my complex feelings but I finally sit here with a sense of hope. Dare I allow myself this privilege? Dare I be happy and have peace? Dare I fully let go of the child inside who had only me to defend her? These are the questions this journey has brought me to and, as I ponder on these, the one word that leaps out to me that all these things require, is the word TRUST.

Trust is gained through being earned. However, we sometimes have to take the risk to choose to trust in order to heal and become strong. Trusting in the Lord is the safest and most assured place to be. The Lord's plan was never for boundaries to be crossed or violated, so when they have been, we find ourselves hiding and running from anyone and everyone, determined never to trust again. We barricade ourselves in and everyone else out, which slowly closes off our heart to our own needs, family, friends, and the Lord, too.

I am choosing to trust again. But I know my full trust can only be in Jesus as anyone else will, in time, invariably let me down. God did not and cannot fail me, and His words can never be spoken without there being mercy, kindness and truth.

To learn to fear God and Him alone is the beginning of wisdom. The fear of God is to understand reverence and the magnitude of who He is. Once we begin to know Him, we see His heart is only ever to do good to us. He's a perfect Father: no weakness, and no harsh demands or punishments.

The love He has for me I am daily learning to give to myself, and He is repairing my identity whilst I am learning the true beauty of who He is, in return.

This is my personal journey, yet there are other journeys, too, that must be taken by others asking these questions: Should I just let it go? Should I report the abuse that happened to me? Is it right if I am supposed to live a life of forgiveness?

I have been asked these questions several times, and I've asked myself the same things. Maybe you are asking the questions, too, as a result of your own experiences.

If we don't report paedophiles, what sort of lawless society would we become? If we stay silent, what will become of the child victim who may be in your family or on the next street to you? Should they be defended and rescued? Should someone in the future be given the opportunity to be safe because a paedophile or rapist was found guilty and put in prison?

The centre of the abused child is rocked, shaken and shattered. The pieces of their heart and identity are trampled on. The child becomes invisible; their needs and their hearts are not seen, and they lose themselves. Maybe this was you. Maybe you were that child. It is never too late to bring into the light what was done to you in the darkness. In most cases of historic sexual abuse, the police told me that the victims who are coming forward are now in their fifties, sixties, seventies and eighties.

The laws of God keep us safe from sin and we, as Christians, cannot ignore them. We wrap them around our hearts for protection.

Equally, the laws of the land are for our safety too, and the reporting of sexual crimes, in my experience, are taken seriously by the police. I know that not all victims of crimes get the result they are looking for, and that is not necessarily because they are not believed or taken seriously but is rather because of a lack of evidence. However, it is not all lost. They have stood for what is true and right and, in my case, I stood and defended a little six-year-old girl, and today I can stand and say that it feels good!

My testimony is that you can live through abuse and trauma and still develop and nurture a beautiful relationship with Jesus while being weak and confused. All this, while bringing to justice the perpetrators of crimes that brought nothing but damage and brokenness into your heart. We must acknowledge the trauma of abuse, and we must get help for it from safe places.

How many times have I needed the help of others to get their shovels out and dig a way through my emotional piles of dung, so I could see a way forward? There has been a LOT of dung...! I cannot do it alone and if I think I can, I've already lost.

A few weeks ago, an old lady, who lives close by, came to see me. She said, "Pippa, do you remember going to a ladies' day in Rochdale twenty years ago?"

"Yes," I replied, intrigued as to what she was going to say. She gave me a piece of paper that she had been given all those years ago on that day.

It read, 'Your heart is safe in my care.'

It pierced my heart. God knew exactly the point where I was struggling. I cried and acknowledged that my Heavenly Father has the safest hands in which I can put my abused, hurting and frightened heart. He knows everything we need before we ask or even recognise that we need it.

My desire for you is within the song that I sing most weeks in church:

I sought the Lord and He heard and He answered.

I was finally seen and heard, and I can be safe in God's hands now. While seeking the Lord, even when your heart is shattered and bearing the scars of trauma, He promises to hear every whisper and every cry. He will answer you because those who put their trust in the Lord will be saved. It is a promise.

You, whoever you are, are fearfully and wonderfully made. You were made to live without fear, to be safe, to be happy and always to have a hope and a future.

That's the plan God has for my life, too. I will not stop letting Him heal my heart, and I will never forget the journey I have been on, but now my memories have built a monument to God: my constant protector and my healer.

# Epilogue

As the waves keep rolling in, the tide, in its time, goes out. This is how my story develops and evolves.

As the old patterns and thoughts change and slowly move away to be left in my past, new waves come, bringing challenges that I had not seen before. I guess this is not the conclusion of the story; in fact, it's just the beginning.

I would like to say that every sadness and trace of damage is gone but, in actual fact, I am walking in new shoes that need bedding in. There will be more challenges and adjustments to make but the one thing I know for certain is that I am not alone and, if you have a similar story, neither are you.

The promise that Jesus gives us, stands. He will perfect that which concerns me...and that is true for you, too.

# I'm Alright...
## I'm Only Hurting

PIPPA RAFAEL

'Shame dies when stories are told in safe places'
Gebhardt Berndt

This is the first part of a true story of how an innocent, Jesus-loving little girl suffered the traumatic sexual abuse at the hands of a close relative and others. Her world was already full of illness, hospitalisation and fear.

As her life unfolded, so did the challenges.

ISBN: 9781913181772

## Restoration of the Abused Heart
*(Winter 2025 release)*

"Restoration of the Abused Heart" takes a deeper look into the compartments of the traumatised heart. Personal stories and experiences are peppered throughout, as I've gone through my own journey with the complex trauma of sexual, spiritual and emotional abuse, alongside the wounds of a long arduous journeys through many medical challenges.

You will be challenged and surprised by the things you didn't know were buried deep inside your heart. It weaves a way through the corridors of a broken heart, restoring understanding, soothing fears, and bringing Jesus into even the darkest of rooms.

It takes an honest look at different coping mechanisms and the roots behind them. By allowing Jesus into every room of your heart you can truly love him with everything you are.